Praise for *The Small Business Money Guide* . . .

"*The Small Business Money Guide* is a must-read for anyone who has started a business or is simply dreaming of doing so. Terri Lonier and Lisa Aldisert have succeeded in writing a book that not only is packed with critical information that can truly make the difference between success and failure for your business, but one that is actually a pleasure to read as well. Consider this book an investment in your business future—it may well be the best one you ever make."

—GINGER APPLEGARTH
Author, *Wake Up and Smell the Money*
and guest financial expert, CNBC

"*The Small Business Money Guide* by Terri Lonier and Lisa Aldisert has a user-friendly format, straightforward language, and a wealth of information that could only have come from two entrepreneurs who have walked the talk. If you're starting your own business, reading this book should be your first investment."

—DAN SULLIVAN
President, The Strategic Coach

"Are you ready to grow your business but need more cash than you've got? Lonier and Aldisert will help you find it with this comprehensive guide for small businesses in growth mode. Particularly helpful are the numerous financial resources listed with addresses, Web sites and phone numbers, and the general overview of business financing. Read this *before* you go to the bank!"

—LINDA STERN
Author, *Money Smart Secrets for the
Self-Employed*

"*The Small Business Money Guide* is an essential companion for any business owner who is serious about being successful in handling money."

—JAN ZOBEL, EA
Tax professional and author, *Minding Her
Own Business: The Self-Employed Woman's
Guide to Taxes and Recordkeeping*

"Terri and Lisa provide real 'how-to' advice about managing business finances and how to get capital. Each chapter is a gold nugget—you can mine the chapters that are of interest to you for real, practical information and knowledge. Read this guide before your start your business, apply for a loan or a line of credit, or choose a bank. Keep it on your desk as a reference for the future as your business grows and your needs change."

—W. KENNETH YANCEY, JR.
Executive Director, SCORE
(Service Corps of Retired Executives)

D1602627

THE
SMALL
BUSINESS
MONEY
GUIDE

Also by Terri Lonier

Books
*Working Solo**
*Working Solo Sourcebook**
*Smart Strategies for Growing Your Business**
The Frugal Entrepreneur

Audio Programs
Working Solo: Getting Started
Working Solo: Getting Customers

* Published by John Wiley & Sons, Inc.

THE
SMALL
BUSINESS
MONEY
GUIDE

HOW TO GET IT, USE IT, KEEP IT

Terri Lonier
Lisa M. Aldisert

JOHN WILEY & SONS, INC.

New York · Chichester · Weinheim · Brisbane · Singapore · Toronto

Copyright © 1999 by Terri Lonier and Lisa M. Aldisert. All rights reserved.

Published by John Wiley & Sons, Inc.
Published simultaneously in Canada.

This publication is designed to provide accurate and authoritative information in regard to the subject matter covered. It is sold with the understanding that the authors and publisher are not engaged in rendering professional services. If professional advice or other expert assistance is required, the services of a competent professional person should be sought.

Working Solo is a registered trademark and The Frugal Entrepreneur is a trademark of Terri Lonier. All other trademarks used in this book are the property of their respective holders.

Library of Congress Cataloging-in-Publication Data:
Lonier, Terri.
    The small business money guide : how to get it, use it, keep it /
  Terri Lonier, Lisa M. Aldisert.
          p.   cm.
    Includes bibliographical references and index.
    ISBN 0-471-24799-5 (pbk. : alk. paper)
      1. Small business—United States—Finance.   I. Aldisert, Lisa M.
  II. Title.
  HG4027.7.L66   1998
  658.15'92—dc21   98-24355
                                                                        CIP

Printed in the United States of America.
10 9 8 7 6 5 4 3 2 1

Photograph of authors: Arthur L. Cohen

May this book encourage entrepreneurs everywhere
to find the money they need to fund
their business dreams.

Preface

If there's one topic that generates the most interest, confusion, and frustration in entrepreneurs, it's money. Business owners know its power—even if they don't clearly understand how it works in their company.

In my encounters with thousands of small business owners over the last 20 years, I've seen first hand the ways that individuals tackle the learning curve about financial matters. To new business owners, money is simple: You make it and you spend it. As a company matures, however, money takes on a different role. Using it as an effective tool for growth requires an understanding of how to get it, manage it, and keep it. Up to now, acquiring that knowledge was difficult and often came with painful trial-and-error experience.

The need for solid, accessible information on financial matters for small business owners was the inspiration for *The Small Business Money Guide*. Its aim is to take the mystery out of money for business owners at every level. I'm pleased to be joined by coauthor Lisa Aldisert, who shares insights on financial matters based on over 20 years of business experience, including 16 years in banking as well as her own entrepreneurial endeavors. Together we've created an easy-to-understand guide to help you master the language and use of money in your business.

This is the first book in the new Working Solo series, a collection designed for businesses that are seeking more in-depth information on specific business topics. Once a company is up and running, where does it turn for the next level of advice? While there are dozens of books devoted to startup issues, few seem to address the pressing issues facing businesses in growth mode. My first book, *Working Solo*, remains the classic startup guide; the Working Solo series brings additional navigation tools to your journey.

We think you'll find this new addition to your Working Solo library one of the best financial investments you can make in your company's future. It comes with our best wishes for your business success.

TERRI LONIER
October 1998

Acknowledgments

A number of people were kind enough to share their wisdom and counsel as we prepared *The Small Business Money Guide*. Lisa would like to acknowledge Tom Boyd, Martha Jewett, Linda Newman, Zach Stein, Bruce Stout, Leigh Talmage, Peggy Yannas, and Ed Zito. She extends thanks to Allegra Blackburn-Dwyer, who assisted her in the research and manuscript preparation. Lisa also expresses great appreciation to her husband, Batt Johnson, for his support and good cheer during the process.

Terri would like to acknowledge Anne Allen, her managing associate, who offered fresh insights about small business financial issues. She extends thanks to her agent, Joe Spieler, and publishing consultant Tom Woll, for their ongoing support of the Working Solo vision and for continuing to ask the deceptively simple questions that bring new perspective. Terri offers a special note of appreciation to her husband, Robert Sedestrom, who has witnessed first hand how entrepreneurs tackle the financial challenges of growing a business.

We also extend our thanks to Mike Hamilton, Laurie Frank, and the entire Wiley publishing team for helping us reach small business owners with the financial information they need.

Contents

SECTION THREE:
MONEY—PREPARING TO GET IT

SECTION FOUR:
MONEY—HOW TO MANAGE IT

SECTION FIVE: MONEY—THE FUTURE

Introduction

When the subject of money or financial management comes up, do you find yourself getting a little anxious? You're in good company. Many small business owners get a little squeamish when they think about financial strategies. Take heart, because there are a lot of myths that have created this unease. Our purpose in writing this book is to demystify the myths surrounding money and to give you some tools and techniques so that you can use money masterfully. We believe everyone can learn these realities, and can immediately implement simple strategies that will result in a stronger business.

The Small Business Money Guide was created for those who are starting or growing a business, and who want to learn more about the financial elements that have such an important impact on a company's success. This book may not make you an expert, but it will give you a framework to discuss financial matters with your banker, your accountant, and your bookkeeper—and with others who work in your company. It will give you more confidence in dealing with issues concerning money.

If you are savvy enough to be an entrepreneur or small business owner, you intuitively know the basics: You are creating products or services for sale to make a profit. That is the essence, and everything else flows from there. Even if your business is more like a hobby, you need to know tips and techniques to manage your cash. If you are serious about growing and running a business and do not have a lot of financial acumen, this book can help fill in the gaps and give you the confidence to make better decisions relating to money.

This book is for you if you want to learn:

✓ How to use money as a management tool
✓ What your chances are to raise money when you need it
✓ Alternative sources of raising money
✓ What obtaining money will cost you

✓ How to anticipate when you will need money

✓ How to package your company for investors

✓ How to clean up your financial act

✓ How to speak the language of money

This book is presented in 50 minichapters so you can get a small dose and quick access to what you need without laboring over technical issues. We recommend that you skim through the book and see which chapters will be particularly helpful for your business. Read the chapters you need to find specific answers; read the whole book and you'll have a valuable money tutorial.

Successful financial management is common sense, combined with an understanding of basic money issues. Small business owners who take a proactive approach end up ahead of their competition and are well positioned for the future. We've designed this book to help you on the journey, and hope that you have fun in the process!

TERRI LONIER   LISA ALDISERT
tlonier@workingsolo.com   moneybook@lisaaldisert.com

MONEY—WHY YOU NEED IT

Chapter 1

What's Your Money Attitude?

oney is a topic that arouses so many emotions in us—excitement and reservation; joy and fear; happiness and sadness; optimism and pessimism. We all have personal feelings about money, and these beliefs affect how we manage money in our businesses. Whether you're starting a business or are growing one, you can't escape money matters.

Money is often a weak link for entrepreneurs and business owners. Chances are, you created a business around an idea, product, or service in which you have particular expertise. You have experience in marketing or manufacturing, but have had less exposure and experience with money management and procedures. You're spending a great deal of time doing what you do best, and know that you need to learn more about financial issues, but don't have the time or inclination to take the next steps.

Your *behavior* about financial matters (that is, *how* you handle money) will make a difference in how effectively and efficiently your business develops over time. But your *values* also have a huge impact on your business, because the values reflect *why* you react to money the way you do.

Consider your personal history. How was money treated in your home? Did your parents convey feelings of scarcity or those of abundance? Were you more of a spender or a saver? Were you given responsibility for money at an early age, or did your parents always handle your money issues? Did you get an allowance? How did you spend it? Did you earn money in your spare time? Were you free to make decisions about what to do with it? Spend some time reflecting on these questions. They'll give you insight into your relationship with money today.

Some people will treat money in the same way as their parents did. Others will take a contrarian view. Understanding your personal history will open the door, but it's up to you to understand the links with your present business. For example, your parents may have had a frugal approach to money when you were growing up. You may copy that in your business, as you understand and agree with your parents' reasons for frugality. Or, you might shun their belief system, thinking that they were miserly in their approach, and "you'll show them." This sort of attitude might result in careless spending in your business that could result in dangerous cash shortfalls.

In contrast to a frugal background, you may have come from a family where the money flowed and you had everything you always wanted. Your adult view may be to freely spend money (feeling that it will always be there). Adopting this attitude in your business might result in a severe cash-flow crisis because you think the money will always be there. On the other hand, you may take the opposite view that money should be saved and not spent. Bringing this attitude into your business could result in not investing in the business as it grows.

We all have entrepreneurial role models who have inspired us. You might have been influenced by more bootstrappers than wealthy executives, for example. But upon looking closer, you'll discover that these entrepreneurs made clear decisions to invest in the business rather than being penny-wise. Their success comes from a balance of committing financial resources to their vision, while simultaneously being frugal where it counts.

Think about the individuals who have inspired you. How do these people handle money? What are their success habits about handling money? How do they compare with the way you handle money in your business? What can you learn from their methods and attitudes?

Successful entrepreneurs do several things when it comes to money matters. First, they know what they know and acknowledge what they don't know. Second, they focus on their stronger competencies and compensate for weaknesses by bringing in advisors who have the missing expertise. Third, they relinquish some control by giving the experts room to make recommendations and decisions. And last, they learn enough about what they don't know in order to effectively communicate with the experts.

The objective is for you to become more comfortable with money as a tool. You will feel empowered by being able to communicate with your financial partners. Having a better understanding of cash flow will make you a better manager—and will help you uncover hidden sources of cash. Your strategic planning process will be enhanced, and you will be able to easily anticipate when you need to raise money.

Our advice as you begin this journey is to loosen up about money. It only becomes a heavy, difficult issue because we make it that way. *The Small Business Money Guide* will break down the money myths and greatly increase your comfort level in dealing with the financial questions about your business.

One last point—remember, we become what we think about. If you *think* you are weak in the money category, then you'll likely stay in that mindset. If you tell people, "I get frazzled when working on money issues," you will continue to be stymied. Changing your attitude is the first step in changing your belief system.

Take our quiz, *Your Money Profile*. You'll learn more about your money belief system, and this will give you a framework for your attitudes and ideology, which directly impact how you handle money in your business.

QUIZ: YOUR MONEY PROFILE

Answer true or false to the following questions:

1. I consistently save money every year for my retirement—even if some years' contributions are smaller than others.

2. I earned money from part-time jobs when I was a child.

3. My parents taught me responsible ways to spend and save my money.

4. I am comfortable discussing financial matters, even though I may not be familiar with all of the technical nuances.

5. In the business, I pay myself first, even when cash is tight.

6. I treat my company's money the same as I treat my personal funds.

7. I have a budget for the next 12 months for my business.

8. I have met the branch manager at my bank.

9. I have a system for tracking the money I receive and the money I spend in the business.

10. I am willing to borrow money to invest in my company's future.

If you answered *true* for 9 to 10 of the statements, you are extremely confident about money matters and have a good foundation of systems in the business. A score of *true* for 7 to 8 of the statements shows that you are on the right track and need to focus on the *false* scores you have control over. If you answered *true* for 5 to 6 of the statements, you need to seek some alliances with people who can help you manage and get more comfortable with the money issues. If you answered *true* to 4 or fewer of the statements, you may need a little more work than other business owners, but remember that money behaviors can be learned.

Chapter 2

How Big Is Your Vision?

W here do you see your business 3, 5, or even 10 years from now? Envisioning your business in the future is one of the success elements that separates you as an achiever from those who merely limp along. If you can visualize your business in the future, you can almost always articulate that vision to others. Having a vision and passionately talking about it are key ingredients of successful entrepreneurs.

It's a good idea to review your business vision once a year. As your company grows, certain nuances will occur and you may end up taking a new direction or emphasizing a different aspect of the business than you did in the beginning. An annual "vision check" will help you maintain perspective and keep you on track.

When you have a good sense of your company's vision, you can set goals to achieve it. Business owners complete goal-planning exercises in many different ways. We recommend you find a process that works for your personality and business, but keep a three-year time horizon in place. Three years is far enough away that you're projecting into the unknown, but it's close enough that you can reach out and virtually touch the end result. By articulating your three-year targets, you can then work backward and set your goals.

How do you create or revisit your vision? A good place to begin is to brainstorm all of the elements that would go into your ideal company, as part of your ideal lifestyle. While our emphasis here is about your business, you know that your business will suffer if you do not have a balance in all aspects of your life. In creating the vision, keep in mind the whole person.

Using the checklist in Figure 2.1 as a guideline, answer each of the questions from the perspective of your ideal vision three years from now. List all of these elements with this important caveat in mind: *Don't edit* any idea that comes up! Record all ideas without judgment as you add them to the list. You may want to share this exercise with anyone who is close to both your business and your personal life.

Figure 2.1

CHARTING YOUR VISION

Creating a vision begins with brainstorming a list of your ideal outcomes for the future. This worksheet is designed to help you clarify your vision. You'll notice that it includes both personal and business issues, since the two are so closely intertwined, particularly in a small business. Take your time completing it, and have fun letting your mind try on different ideas. The process takes place in three steps.

Step 1. First, imagine it is three years from today. Jot down ideas for the *best-case scenario* of what you would like your life to be like by answering the following questions. All responses are appropriate—don't edit or make any judgments at this time. (If you need more room, feel free to do this planning on separate sheets of paper.)

1. Where are you living? What is your lifestyle like?

2. Describe your relationships with friends and family.

3. What do you do with your leisure time?

4. What do you do for personal growth?

5. How do you contribute to your community?

6. What does your business look like? What type of work are you doing? How big is the business?

7. What does your personal financial picture look like?

(Continued) ➠

Step 2. Once you've answered the questions, review them and evaluate each item based on the *reality check* of them occurring in the next three years. Then prioritize the items in the order of importance to you, based on your own personal values.

Here are the things I'd like to do within the next three years that are important to me, rated in order of priority:

1.

2.

3.

4.

5.

6.

7.

8.

9.

10.

(Continued) ➡

8

Step 3. The final step in charting your vision is to write a description of your life three years from now. Write it in as much detail as you can, including all the aspects you've mentioned in Step 1 and Step 2. Also, write it in the present tense (not the future), as if all of your goals have already come to pass. For example, use phrases such as "I am living . . ." or "I am working . . ." instead of "I will be living . . ." or "I will be working. . . ."

It is three years from today, and this is what my life is like:

After you have made the list, it is time for some reality checks. Remember—you are not developing the *worst-case* scenario, rather you are creating the *best-case* scenario. First, evaluate each item based on the possibility of its occurrence in the next three years. After doing this, prioritize the items in order of their importance to you. Here is where you need to be aware of your personal values. If you prioritize the list in a way that is consistent with your belief system, you have a much higher probability of achieving the vision. If you are out of sync, on the other hand, you will constantly struggle—largely on a subconscious basis—with the vision of your life and business against your values and beliefs.

Everyone's unique experiences add to the creation of the vision. By understanding what makes you tick, you will be able to create and achieve a vision that is consistent with who you are. If you are driven to make as much money as you can, your vision will reflect that. Achieving that vision will be likely if your values parallel your desire for money. But if you would rather give away all of your money to charity, a vision of making a lot of money won't be congruent (unless, of course, you are driven to *make* a lot of money so that you can *give away* a lot of money).

Once you've evaluated your list and determined that it's in sync with who you are, write a page describing the vision. In writing this, include all the aspects just mentioned. The end result will be a descriptive view of your life three years from now, including what your business looks like and how it fits within your life.

By now you may be asking, "How does all of this vision talk relate to money?" That's easy—*it takes money to make money.* If you have a solid view of where you are going and how it fits into your overall lifestyle, then you can look at how much money it's going to take to get there. Start with the vision, then develop goals to achieve it. Your use of money is one of the tools that will help you get to where you want to go. By having a clear plan, you will know how to anticipate when your business will need money.

When you are able to clearly articulate the vision for your business, you will see that managing cash flow and raising money for specific purposes are two tools that will help you reach the desired goal. Your attitudes about money will creep into the equation as you formulate your vision—your willingness to use money as a tool may indeed make a huge difference in successfully attaining that vision.

Be careful how you edit the money issues here. If you think you have a great product and can easily raise external money regardless of the financial condition of your company, then you are not being realistic. An opposite scenario is also worth mentioning: You're doing all of the "right things" with your business, but resist raising money you need to grow it because you think debt is bad. That attitude can hold you back just as easily as having sloppy, unprofessional systems.

Managing and raising money are important keys to growing your business and achieving your vision. Taking the time to define your vision, and identifying the appropriate ways to use money as a tool, are essential steps in making that vision come true.

Chapter 3

Reasons to Borrow Money

Once you've decided that your company needs external financing, where do you begin? First, you need to step back and identify the *purpose* for borrowing the funds. Investors want to know *why* you want the money and *how* you will repay it. It really is that simple, but many business owners are not prepared to clearly answer the *why* and *how*.

Since you may have several needs for financing, it's best to make a list of them. Some types of financing may be a better match for specific business needs than others. Let's take a look at some of your options.

Short-term or long-term? Think about whether you need to borrow for day-to-day aspects of your business, or to create a better or more efficient product or service in the future. The first type is typically a *short-term* need (in banker parlance, the funds will be needed for less than one year), whereas the second type is a *long-term* need (greater than one year).

Understanding the short- or long-term need will help in your planning process. Short-term loans are really advances against payments that you have not yet received from your customers—for example, invoices you've sent out that haven't been paid to you yet. They are technically self-liquidating—that is, the loans are repaid once *you* get paid. For example, your customer owes you money, but you need to pay bills, so you borrow what you need. When your customer pays up, you repay the loan that was used to pay your bills. In contrast to these self-liquidating short-term loans, long-term loans typically finance equipment or property, or other assets that are more permanent in nature.

There are many reasons why business owners borrow money. Here are some of the more common ones:

Startup financing. You have a great idea for a business and have no money to implement this great idea. What you need is *seed capital*, or *startup financing*.

It is highly unlikely that you will get this money from a bank. Instead, look to friends, family, and angels to give you the money to get started. (We'll be covering this in Chapters 6 and 14.)

Working capital loans.   Do you have cash-flow mismatches, such as needing money to pay bills because you have not yet been paid by your customers? You need *working capital.* Your cash shortfalls may range from paying suppliers to paying your rent to paying your employees. Working capital loans are for short-term needs and are related to the cycle of creating, selling, and collecting money from the sale of your product or service. When you borrow for working capital, it is expected that the loans will be paid back within a short period of time (for example, 30 to 90 days).

Financing capital expansion.   Do you need money to buy a major piece of production equipment to enhance your manufacturing capabilities? Or perhaps you want to expand your facilities to accommodate more production? You need a loan for *capital expansion.* Loans for capital equipment are structured to be repaid over a number of years. The repayment schedule takes into account the useful life of the property or equipment as well as the increased product sales that will be generated by putting it in use.

Equipment leasing.   If you are in a service business, you won't need equipment to manufacture your product, but perhaps you need to overhaul your computer and telecommunications systems. This is also a capital equipment decision, and you may purchase it with the funds from a long-term loan. You may also decide to *lease* the equipment. An evaluation of the lease versus loan option with your banker will help you decide the best course of action. The lease payments will match the useful life of the equipment. (You'll learn more about leasing in Chapter 12.)

Acquisition financing.   You've grown your business nicely, and you see an opportunity to double your sales by purchasing another company. The only problem is that you don't have the money to buy this company, so you need acquisition financing. This is a type of long-term financing. The decision to lend you money will be based on your company's financial condition as well as that of the company you are buying.

Real estate financing.   You see an opportunity to buy a building that you can use in the business. It will be a great investment for your company, so you decide to buy instead of rent. A commercial real estate loan, secured through a mortgage on the building, will finance your purchase.

Bridge financing.   This is usually connected with the simultaneous purchase and sale of property or companies. You may be purchasing a new property that will be paid for with the proceeds of the sale of the old property. The timing may be somewhat mismatched, though, and you may need to close on the new property prior to closing the sale that will generate the funds. Bridge financing "bridges" the gap between those two transactions, and is obtainable if iron-clad agreements are in place to ensure that the lender will not be stuck with an albatross if the first deal doesn't come to fruition.

Business expansion.   Perhaps you want to expand your business into a new area and need to raise money to finance this growth. This kind of financing is also long-term in nature, and will depend, among other variables, on whether you're starting from scratch in the expansion, or if you're buying a business already operating in the area that interests you. If you're starting from scratch, the lenders will look at it with a similar view as to a startup, and your history and track record in the area of expertise will be critical. If you're buying an existing company, it will be considered acquisition financing.

Project financing.   Suppose your company is hired by a large corporation as an outsourced specialist for a big project. The project will take 18 months between the design and implementation stages, and you may need to hire extra contractors or purchase additional equipment to successfully complete it. You will need to borrow money, but don't want to tap into your working capital line of credit for this project, as it would drain your credit available for day-to-day needs. In this case, you may obtain a special project loan that would be structured around the specific characteristics and life of the project. In setting up the loan, lenders will look at what your cash flow needs will be at different stages of the project.

As you can see, there are many reasons businesses borrow money. Keep in mind, however, that no matter what you intend to use the funds for, you'll need to have a clear idea of *why* you need the money and *how* you will repay it. Those are the basic issues for most lenders, and being well prepared to answer them will show that you have thought through the implications of your request. Lenders must always answer to someone else, and among the first questions they'll ask you will be the *why* and *how.* Before you meet with a lender, do your homework and be ready to address these two issues. It can make the difference in getting your funding—and in the success of your business.

Chapter 4

Starting Your Business

A nyone who has ever launched a business knows about the thrill that comes with turning an idea into reality. Many entrepreneurs start with a product or service that they have either manufactured, marketed, sold, or delivered for someone else. They figure out how to "build a better mousetrap," and voilà, they find themselves in business.

Sound familiar? There are many successful entrepreneurs who started this way, and most will tell you that a bit more forethought would have made their early business days easier, and enabled them to avoid many problems.

There are many resources available to help you launch a business. Our goal here is to highlight those related to money and starting a business. You'll notice that a number of the ideas are things best done *before* leaving your day job. But even if you're already out on your own, it's never too late to act upon a good idea.

Preparing to take the plunge. If you work for someone else and have an inkling that you want to go into business for yourself, start saving money. Save as much as you can—some experts say that you should save six months' worth of expenses to cover the risky startup phase. A more conservative view is to set aside one to two years' worth of expenses.

Ready to go and haven't saved a dime? You can still pull it off if your idea is good enough and you have enough passion. But the road of the ultrabootstrapper is a tough one. If your idea is only average and you have little passion for it, save yourself the stress of going into business and struggling from day one. Being in business for yourself requires enormous discipline, drive, and fortitude, and it won't work if you don't have the passion and desire to pull it off.

Is it just an idea or is it really a business? Have you thought through this great idea of yours? Have you researched the market for this product, your ability to sell it, and your ability to get financing? In a nutshell, have you developed a business plan? The process of creating a business plan (Chapter 30) will reveal a lot. For example, you may have a wonderful idea that doesn't translate into a business because it requires capital that you don't have. In that case, you will need to create a prototype (which takes money) to demonstrate its real marketability. Or, you may have a service business that requires capital for increased staffing or equipment. Thinking through your business idea and creating a plan are important steps—don't gloss over them.

Cash flow and capitalization.   A number of small business experts talk about the high percentage of businesses that fail due to inadequate capitalization. This may be the case for many companies, but we suggest broadening the concept: a high percentage of small businesses fail because their owners don't have a clue about managing cash flow. As a rule of thumb, service businesses (those where you are renting out your brain or skills for a fee) require less capital than product businesses (those where you are making a product for sale). Do your homework about minimum levels of capital for your business by networking with other business owners and by talking to your accountant and banker.

Capitalization *is having adequate financial muscle to get you through the startup phase of your business.* **Cash flow** *is the money that comes in and out of the business on a regular basis. A business needs enough capitalization to get up and running, but steady, positive cash flow is what allows a business to survive.*

Cash-flow issues will exist over the life of a company, and you'll get your first dose when you start the business. Keep track of every dollar you bring in and every dollar you spend. Create a budget and track your revenue and expense levels compared to the budget (see Chapter 41). The sooner you get into the habit of tracking your cash, the more you will be prepared to handle the unexpected events that can throw your cash flow into a tail spin—and your business into the danger zone.

Pricing your product or service.   This is another area of stress for startup entrepreneurs. Correctly pricing your product or service directly affects your revenue numbers. If you *underprice*—a syndrome of many startup entrepreneurs—you need to generate more volume just to cover your expenses. If you *overprice,* the market will respond by not buying. Either way, it's a problem. Again, this is about doing your homework. Research how your competition is priced and see what range is reasonable from the market perspective.

Create a network of money pros.   Don't wait until you've been in business a year before you find an accountant, an insurance broker, and a banker. Network around at the first opportunity so that you're ready to engage these professionals early on in your business. If you partner with them from the beginning, and treat them as extended members of your management team, they'll be invaluable to your business.

Rainy day protection.   Starting your business with your personal expenses covered is one way to protect yourself. But have you thought about what happens if you become disabled once the business gets going and you can't pay your company's bills? Business interruption insurance is one possibility, which we discuss in Chapter 44. The other is to have a personal disability policy in place. Get one while you still have your day job. If you wait until after you are in business, you won't be eligible until you can prove that you are consistently taking home a certain salary.

Obtaining personal credit.   Again, this is something to work on before you leave your day job. If you want to refinance your mortgage, get a home equity line, obtain additional credit cards—whatever the financial need—do it while you are still working for someone else. Once you are on your own, your personal credit capacity drops dramatically in the eyes of the banker. You'll need three years of tax returns once you are in business to prove that you make enough money to support a mortgage or a refinancing.

Credit cleanup.   If you have time to prepare, clean up your personal credit before going into business. (We'll cover more specifics in Chapter 28.) A good personal credit history will always be to your advantage when you need to borrow money.

When you're launching a business, there's an endless set of details to pay attention to—and we're the first to admit that sitting down to realistically assess your money needs is not one that tops most entrepreneurs' lists. However, the more money prepping you do before getting started, the more effective you'll be in those important early days of your business.

Chapter 5

Money for Managing and Growing Your Business

After you've passed the startup stage, your money focus will shift to managing and growing your business. Managing your business involves a lot of focus on cash flow, while growing your business often adds the dynamic of raising money.

Top line or bottom line?   One of the most common pieces of business advice is to *watch the bottom line.* What exactly does this mean? The substance behind bottom-line management is to manage (meaning *moderate* or *cut*) expenses in order to raise net profits. While it is obviously important to keep a close eye on expenses as part of the management process, we think small business owners need to think just as much about the *top* line—the revenue (sales) generated—as the company grows. *Your job as the owner/entrepreneur is to use your specific talents to generate more revenue.* Both top- and bottom-line management will affect your company's cash flow. It's up to you to decide which is more important at your current stage of growth. *Both* are important.

---

*Focusing on your **top line** means that you're putting energy into building your revenue, such as increasing sales. When you're watching out for your **bottom line**, you're trying to keep your expenses under control.*

Self-employed versus enterprise.   Are you building a business, or are you in business for yourself? It's a subtle, but important, distinction. If you're in a service business where you are essentially renting yourself out as a consultant, there's a limit to how much time you can work and, as a result, to how much revenue you can generate. The consultant who gets paid only by fees for services rendered is actually *self*-employed—it's just like a job. He or she needs to actually render consulting services in order to make money. If you add products into the mix, however, you have the foundation of building a business, and you increase the opportunity to grow both the top and bottom lines. Of course, the choice to expand your business in this way is up to you. What's important is to understand the financial limits that come with running a business based only on billing for your time.

Size isn't everything.   As you contemplate growing your business, another important concept to keep in mind is that bigger is not necessarily better. Many people do not understand this: They run multi-million-dollar companies that seem to exist simply to support the people who work for the company. How could that happen? It's easier than you think. People get caught up in the perceived glamour of the bigger size, and they lose sight of what really counts. Focus on *what you keep,* not what you gross!

Cash is king.   As you manage the business, your money issues will all revolve around cash flow. Even if the business has grown to the size where you employ a controller or treasurer, as the business owner you need to be completely in tune with the pattern of how money enters and exits your company. Sadly, many entrepreneurs completely delegate this responsibility to a financial person only to find out later what poor financial shape their company is in—or worse yet, they learn about embezzlement or false record keeping. You can prevent this situation by staying current with your firm's financial issues on a regular basis. For example, one entrepreneur we know owns a $2-million training company. He boasts that he receives a cash-flow spreadsheet *daily*—he reviews it and knows exactly what's going on in his business. What we found interesting is that he doesn't view himself as a "money person." But he knows that he needs to monitor these daily reports in order to be on top of what's going on in his firm. Proactive cash management is a tool to help you grow your business, and we'll talk about this in more detail in later chapters.

The money treadmill.   Many entrepreneurs feel that they cannot keep up with the money cycle—they find it to be a constant struggle of managing cash flow. It's imperative to take a hard look at all of your major expense categories and objectively evaluate how your money is working for the business.

One common issue is a great reluctance to add staff "because it costs too much." Before you disregard the idea of staff, take time to think about how much it's costing you to do lower-level activities that could be done by someone else at a lesser wage. Is your time best utilized packing product for shipment, or going to the post office? Hire someone at a modest wage to do this and it will free you to do what you do best. Again, think of this as building a company rather than being all on your own.

Your legacy.   As the business grows, your focus will shift to other new concerns. For example, do you want to be known for superb quality, or as the lowest-cost producer? Both are great objectives, but it is virtually impossible for one company to be excellent at both. Whichever you choose as priorities, you'll have to find funding to support them. As you evaluate the direction of the business, pay careful attention to what kind of investment will be necessary to attain your goals. This can be investment in people, products, equipment—it doesn't matter for what as long as you have a strategy for raising and repaying the money.

It's also important to invest in some quality strategic planning time as your business grows. Become clear on what you are *really* seeking in exchange for taking on debt. Are you buying market share? Diversification of a product line? Top-line growth? More efficient facilities to produce the product? Higher quality staff to service the product? State-of-the-art systems to maximize efficiency?

Know what you are really after—and see if it fits within your primary objective of quality product, excellent customer service, or lowest-cost producer. Rank what's important, and realize that you can't be all things to all people. If your goal is to provide the best customer service, for example, investing in facilities and equipment to become the lowest-cost producer doesn't make sense.

Return on investment.   As you borrow more money, you'll spend more time thinking about the cost of capital and return on investment. In the beginning—when you have fewer choices—a loan with a high interest rate is better than no loan at all. After your company has established a track record and has demonstrated a proven ability to repay, you'll have more options available. As you evaluate cost of capital, you'll find yourself shifting your thinking from "We need this money to survive" to "Will the company be receiving a satisfactory return on investment by borrowing money for this particular project?" Different stages, different objectives.

---

*Your **cost of capital** is the cost of getting the money you need. In its simplest sense, it represents the interest expense on loans or the dividends paid on shares of your stock. Savvy business owners are always evaluating the tradeoff of what they must pay or give up to get the money, against the benefits of what the money will bring their firm.*

Financial partners.   Another thing to think about as the business grows is whether your financial partners are serving your business in the same way as when you started. In some cases, you may be able to grow with your original accounting firm or bank, but in other cases it makes more sense to engage in new relationships with those who are better equipped to support your growth. Network with other business owners whose companies are of similar size and focus to make some new connections. And, continue to support your former financial partners by referring business to them that fits their ideal client targets. Remember, you never know when you may be starting another venture and they may be the perfect partners for you again.

Understanding cash flow and knowing how to use money as a tool are two things that separate successful entrepreneurs from those who just limp along. Learn what you can and supplement your knowledge with help from competent financial professionals.

MONEY—WHERE TO GET IT

Chapter 6

Easy Money Sources for Startups

How do I find money to start my business? This is the most frequently asked question from startup entrepreneurs. Most of us don't enjoy the luxury of a million-dollar idea that mints money from day one. On the contrary, we typically have *good, untested* ideas that we *believe* we can make into a business. Unfortunately, *good* is not great, *untested* means no proof, and *believe* is not fact.

The basic premise of an investment is to receive a return. This comes in the form of interest on a loan, dividends or capital appreciation from stock, interest on bonds, and so forth. At the beginning, we have no track record, no customer base—essentially no credibility—when it comes to going to strangers and asking for money. That is why the likeliest bet at the beginning is to go to the people who know you best: your family and friends.

Your company, your cash. Before going to mom and dad, though, let's talk about you. If you go to a bank or other institution for money, the first thing they're going to ask is how much *you* are investing in the business. Your answer might be that you have no cash—you're contributing your blood and sweat to make the venture viable. Sweat equity, as this is called, is important but not compelling. In the eyes of the investor, you have nothing tangible to lose if you donate "only" your efforts but no cash. The same thing applies, although to a lesser extent, to friends and family. They want to see that you are financially on the hook also.

Sweat equity *is a person's contribution of their physical effort—in essence, their "blood, sweat, and tears"—into a business, instead of money.*

So, get clear on the fact that you're going to invest some of your own money in your venture. You will find that your level of commitment changes substantially when you write that check. While it is quite sobering to invest cash in your idea, it's also highly motivating and exhilarating. You'll empower yourself by putting your hard-earned money on the line.

Good news, bad news.   It's actually the same news: asking friends and family to fund your business. You must understand that this is about *you* first, your company second. These folks who have known and loved you are investing in *you.* It's your energy, enthusiasm, intelligence, creativity, marketing ability, business acumen—whatever they perceive as your genius—that they're investing in.

The specifics of your business venture are new to everyone. The difference between your family and friends and the strangers at a bank is their knowledge and insight about you, your character, your level of responsibility, and other personal factors. If all of those stack up, they're going to take the risk in investing in your business because they believe in you (and your idea) and they want to support your venture from the beginning.

The upside of this relationship is that they will forgive you for your faults. The downside is that they can also potentially blast you for them. If your company does well, they may act like they own it. If it fails, they may blame you for not telling them about the potential risks of the venture.

Family.   This is a very tricky subject because of all of the emotions connected to these relationships. If you already have a highly volatile relationship with the person who has the purse strings, you need to think through the implications of asking for money for your business. Chances are that a borrower/investor relationship may make such a relationship even more explosive. You may think that the risk is worth it, but it is important to carefully think through all possible outcomes.

Friends.   When borrowing from friends, the implications are essentially the same as family, with a few subtle differences. Your good friend, Dave, may be a great guy with whom you have a terrific relationship. Upon having his money in hand, you may see an entirely different, excitable person who could drive you nuts after the first week. In most family relationships, you can often anticipate any emotional reactions from taking money. You may have more surprises with friends.

Setting the stage.   Have a heart-to-heart talk with your potential investors about your mutual expectations in this arrangement. In addition to telling them all of the wonderful aspirations for the business, also share the downside risks. Find out if they are interested in being silent financial partners, or if they want more active roles. Are you willing to give them more active participation if they ask? How often do they want to hear from you? What sort of reports, if any, do they expect from you? While it may be unpleasant, you should discuss the potential downside—for example, how will your inability to repay affect your relationship?

If you discuss all of this ahead of time, it will minimize the challenge of dealing with problems as the business grows. Be direct, honest, and sincere in your comments and treat your new investors with the same respect you would provide any stranger who lends you money. Be sure to clarify your relationship. And, please *document* any investment to protect all involved parties: you, your company, and your family members.

Types of investments. Friends and family investments can be loans, equity, or gifts. In any case, you want to have a formal record of the transaction. If it is a gift, the investor can give $10,000 per year without incurring any tax. If it is equity, you will issue stock in your company in exchange for the investment. Ask your attorney to review your articles of incorporation and advise you on the best way to structure an equity investment. If your company is structured as an S corporation, you want to make sure that issuing stock will not compromise the S status.

If the investment is a loan, decide whether it is a personal loan to you, or a loan to the company. Then create a promissory note (an IOU) to document the loan. Consult your certified public accountant (CPA) to make sure that the interest rate passes the Internal Revenue Service (IRS) minimum interest rate test so your family member avoids any potential income tax or gift problems. The IRS has guidelines on minimum interest rates depending on the type and intent of the loan.

Sometimes funding can come from unexpected sources, as demonstrated in the story of Ellen, an entrepreneur we know. Ellen designs and manufactures women's clothes and had no intention of asking any family members for money when she started her business. She was surprised when they came to her, unsolicited, offering to help. She gratefully accepted their offer and agreed upon a loan structure. Her company issued a five-year promissory note to each investor, which simply stated that her company would repay the debt and the terms of the repayment. Her family members then lent the money and were paid an interest rate of prime plus 3 percent, with interest payable semiannually.

Prime *is the interest rate that banks charge their corporate customers. It is published daily in newspapers such as the* Wall Street Journal.

In the second year, Ellen was unable to meet one of the interest payments, and advised each person in advance, in writing, about the situation. Each of them waived the interest payment until her business's cash flow improved. Ellen's approach may seem formal, but she wanted the business side of her relationship with family members to be just that: business.

Having family and friends as investors can be an emotional roller coaster, but in the beginning it may be your only viable option. To make it work, keep personal and business conversations separate, and treat these well-meaning individuals with the same respect you would any business partner. Communication is key, so don't forget to keep them informed about your business once you have their money. In addition to being investors, you'll find they may also become your greatest cheerleaders as you build your business.

AN INVESTOR PRIMER

When it's time to search for funding for your new or growing business, the terminology can be confusing. Here are some definitions to help you communicate better with financial professionals.

An *investor* is a company or person who provides your company with *debt* or *equity* capital. *Debt* represents money that is *lent* to the company, to be paid back under specified terms and conditions with interest. Investors who lend money are usually referred to as *lenders*, such as banks, credit unions, finance companies, factors, and savings or thrift institutions, as well as friends and family.

In exchange for the use of the lender's money, your company is promising to repay the debt along with predetermined interest. The riskier the loan, the higher the interest rate. The higher rate is to compensate the lender for the higher level of risk. If the company is unable to repay the debt, it is in *default*.

Loans are either *secured* or *unsecured*. Secured loans require a pledge of *collateral,* which is an asset (something you own) greater than or equal to the value of the loan. Unsecured loans, on the other hand, do not require collateral. Real estate lending is an example of a typical secured loan: The lender advances a loan which is secured by the underlying property (a mortgage). Banks often require collateral from growing companies that have little track record as borrowers, since they view them as greater risks.

Equity is an *ownership* interest, typically in the form of common or preferred stock. This stock may pay *dividends* or may be held for capital appreciation (an increase in value of what you own). When an investor purchases equity in your company, he or she will then own a specified percentage of your company. Your company is under no legal obligation to redeem the shares at a later time: If the company goes under, the investor has lost his or her investment.

Chapter 7

Leveraging Your Personal Credit

When you're looking for money to start or expand your business, it sometimes takes creativity to find some cash. If you're going to tap into your own personal reserves, the two best places to start are from your savings and personal credit sources. If you're able to withdraw cash with no penalty, then savings can be a great resource. If your money is tied up, then you need to dig a little deeper.

Savings. If you have a savings account, certificates of deposit (CDs), mutual funds, stocks, or bonds, you can cash in these investments fairly easily and use the money to invest in your business immediately. This works best if the timing is right and you won't be penalized by cashing in prior to a rollover date. You may be penalized, however, for prematurely redeeming investments in retirement vehicles, such as Individual Retirement Accounts (IRAs) or Keoghs, which we'll explore in Chapter 8.

Use savings as collateral. Perhaps you have money invested in a CD that matures nine months from now, and you don't want to be penalized for early withdrawal. Most banks will allow you to borrow money on your own personal credit, and pledge the CD as collateral. When the CD matures, you can use the proceeds to pay off the personal loan. Ask your banker about the logistics of this sort of borrowing. In this case, there is a clear connection that the CD is collateral that will be used to repay the loan when the CD matures.

Credit cards. Get a group of small business owners together to talk about funding a business, and chances are high that stories will fly about using credit cards as startup or expansion funds. Credit cards are one of the most popular ways small business owners gather the cash they need to get their businesses off the ground. These days consumer credit is widely available, and if your personal credit is decent, you're probably receiving frequent credit card solicitations in the mail.

Success stories abound of how someone used 10 credit cards to start up a business, and it became a multi-million-dollar business "overnight." One entrepreneur who owns an advertising agency in the Midwest said that if it hadn't been for the multiple credit card applications both he and his wife tapped into to get their agency going, they wouldn't have their successful business today.

What stories like these don't reveal, however, are the substantial risks that come with leveraging your personal credit. For every successful credit card risk taker, there are also numerous small business owners who ended up losing their business as well as all their personal belongings because they got swept away in the tidal wave of debt. So while using credit cards to finance a business seems quick and easy, it's also important to be very clear about the potential danger. Before you sign up for new cards, here are some things to keep in mind:

- ✓ Credit card debt is expensive. After the short, reduced-rate introductory offer period expires, you'll be facing steep interest rates that consume a lot of cash.

- ✓ Every time you apply for and receive a new credit card, it is reported to the credit bureau and your overall credit capacity declines. If you accept the offers on five new credit cards and never use them, the credit bureau still calculates your credit capacity based on all five cards being used to their full limits. The lesson here is to *not* get them if you don't really need them.

- ✓ If you do use credit cards for business, don't commingle business and personal expenses on the same card. Keep the business expenses separate so that they are documented for tax purposes.

- ✓ Remember that this is your personal credit we are addressing here. Loading up on cards may give you the much-needed cash to rev up your business. But if you aren't able to maintain at least the minimum monthly payment, you're risking your personal credit rating. This will come back to haunt you at a later time when you're trying to get a bank loan.

Many people use credit cards to finance their businesses because they think they're not eligible for other forms of debt. Don't assume this. You may be pleasantly surprised to see that your business does qualify for a bank loan—and you'll save hundreds of dollars in interest expense over the course of the year.

Having too many credit cards often leads to an out-of-control situation with both your personal and business credit. People find themselves robbing Peter to pay Paul, and sometimes they get caught in the vicious cycle of borrowing under one card to pay the minimum balance on another. If you've had challenges in your personal credit history in the past, be very careful how you handle credit cards. Many people get so overwhelmed that they can't think clearly as a result. Is it worth risking your business to put yourself in that situation? Only you can answer that question. Make sure you clearly consider the risk as well as the rewards.

Home equity lines.   If you own your home, you may be eligible to apply for a home equity line, which is in effect a second mortgage on your home. For example, your home may be currently appraised at $230,000, with an underlying mortgage balance of $150,000. Lenders who make available home equity lines of credit may use the benchmark, for example, of a 75-percent loan-to-value ratio, meaning they will lend up to 75 percent of the value of the property. In this case that amount is $172,500, and after subtracting the first mortgage amount of $150,000, the difference of $22,500 is the amount of the new home equity line.

A **loan-to-value ratio** *is a number, often expressed as a percentage, that a lender uses to calculate a loan collateralized by an asset. For example, if a lender uses a loan-to-value ratio of 90%, and you have a home or office building valued at $100,000, your maximum loan would be 90% of $100,000, or $90,000.*

Once the $22,500 is approved and available to you, you can draw down on any amount up to $22,500, as needed. The benefit of this arrangement is that you don't need to borrow any of it until you need it; therefore, no interest is charged until you actually borrow the money.

Applying for a home equity line is similar to applying for a mortgage, meaning the bank will take an appraisal of your property, and you will have to file a credit application. Your current earning power and credit rating will have an impact on the decision.

If you're thinking about starting a business at some later time, it makes sense to apply for the home equity line while you still have your day job. You won't need to borrow until you need it, and it will be there waiting for you.

Home equity lines were created as a way of financing home improvements, not for funding new business loans, so two risks must be mentioned. First, if your personal earnings suffer due to growing the business, you may find it very difficult to make your payments on both the mortgage *and* the home equity line. If you default on these for a few months, you're in serious danger of losing your home.

Second, if the market value of your home seriously declines, you may find yourself in a precarious situation. This can happen if you buy the house at the top of the real estate cycle, and then the market goes down, and the value of your house goes down with it. If you need to sell your house in a hurry, the value may be less than the debt you owe, meaning that you will have to come up with additional money to sell your house. Using our previous example, if the house was sold for $165,000, you would be responsible for repaying the entire $172,500. Your inability to do so would jeopardize your personal credit for years to come.

Other personal loans.   Many people have personal lines of credit available at banks or credit unions. These resources can be used as well. Make sure you know the minimum payment requirements so that you continue to be a customer in good standing.

In the early stages of business growth, many owners must rely on using their own assets and personal credit to create cash for the company. This is due, in part, because the company itself has not built up any credit rating or reputation—and in many cases the individual and the company are one and the same.

If you're facing this situation, you must ask yourself how much you're willing to compromise your own personal credit rating in order to take your business to the next level. One serious setback today could be a glaring spot on your credit report for years to come. We're not saying that it's not worth the risk—we just want you to think through any decisions that will affect your personal credit going forward.

Chapter 8

Digging Deeper into Your Personal Financial Assets

In the last chapter we started digging into sources of cash from your personal savings and personal credit. In this chapter, we continue searching, and explore some less common ways to find cash from your assets.

Leverage your brokerage account. If you have money invested in stocks, bonds, or mutual funds, you may be able to borrow money using these investments as collateral. This happens in a *margin account* through your brokerage firm. You will fill out an application for a margin account and, upon approval, you can pledge any stocks, bonds, or mutual funds—your *securities*—as collateral to borrow money. (You do not automatically receive margin privileges when you set up a brokerage account, so check with your broker.)

Securities *are stocks or bonds. A* **margin account** *allows you to borrow money by using securities you own as collateral. Borrowing against securities is risky during periods when the stock market is volatile, since you are responsible for the entire amount you borrowed, even if your securities lose value.*

The purpose of margin credit is to allow you as a brokerage customer to buy additional securities, or to borrow money secured by those securities. The risks of borrowing on margin occur when the market value of your investments declines. So using a margin loan is not a great idea during a volatile period in the stock market.

Let's take a closer look at how this may work. Say you own $20,000 worth of stock that you do not want to sell yet. But you do need the cash, so you decide to take a margin loan, which is usually 50 percent of the market value of the stock. This loan is automatically repaid when you sell the stock. In this example, you would be able to borrow $10,000, secured by the $20,000 of stock. This is a relatively low-risk transaction unless the value of your stock plunges quickly. Using our example, if you have borrowed $10,000 and the value of the stock decreased to $15,000, the broker would issue what is called a *margin call.* You would either need to repay $2,500 on the loan (bringing it back to a 50-percent value), or the brokerage firm would have the right to sell your stock to repay the part of the loan that is under water.

As you can see, this type of borrowing is not for the faint of heart. But if you have securities that you feel are relatively stable (that you don't want to sell yet), a margin loan is one option to get cash for your business.

Retirement accounts.   Many people have IRA or 401(k) accounts. In theory, this money cannot be used until you reach age 59½; prior to that time, you will pay a penalty of 10 percent, plus income taxes on the amount you withdraw. This can obviously be a steep price to pay, but many business owners do break into their retirement plans because they feel they have no other choice. By doing so, they are making the decision to forego the future benefit of the retirement money to have it today to fund their dream. The payoff, of course, comes if the business is a huge financial success and the amount taken from the retirement fund is replaced many times over from the profits of the company.

A new retirement option is a Roth IRA, which taxes contributions when they are made, allowing the funds to grow tax-free. Once a Roth IRA has been in place for 5 years, those over 59½ or disabled may withdraw money without penalty and without paying income taxes. Because Roth IRAs are relatively new, you should check with your financial professional on your eligibility and on how you can maximize the benefits of a Roth IRA for your specific needs.

Retirement accounts are tax advantaged to provide incentives for people to save for their future. We do not know what kind of availability there will be under Social Security 20, 30, or even 50 years from now. Taking responsibility for our future financial security is what a retirement plan is all about. Know that if you use it today, you may regret not having it later.

If you have an IRA or other retirement account and would like to withdraw some or all of the money, get in touch with the bank or brokerage firm that services your account to find out about any penalties. You can locate the contact information on your quarterly summary statement.

If you're working for a company where you participate in a 401(k) plan, you have less flexibility. You won't be able to cash in your plan, but there may be situations where the plan allows borrowings against it for what are called *hardship loans.* These are usually for medical emergencies or to fund college tuition. Ask your human resources or benefits specialist about the specifics, and see if you are eligible for any hardship borrowings.

Keep in mind that you are paying a steep price when you borrow under your 401(k). While paying prime plus 1 percent may be appropriate when you are borrowing from a bank, it is a high price to pay to borrow from yourself. By borrowing under a 401(k), you are paying twice: once for the interest and once for the penalty.

Life insurance policies.   If you own a whole life insurance policy that has a cash value, you can borrow usually up to 90 percent of the cash value at a very attractive interest rate. In today's environment, many people buy term life insurance instead of whole life, as it is a much cheaper alternative in the earlier years. Whole life costs more, but it does build up a cash value that you can use in times when you need the cash. If a loan has been taken against an insurance policy and the policyholder dies with the loan still due, the death benefit is reduced by the outstanding loan amount. (We'll be talking more about whole life and term life insurance in Chapter 44.)

Talk to your insurance representative about borrowing options. Or call the company's customer service phone number (located on your statement) to get specific information. Loans up to a certain amount often can be approved over the phone. Once you've done what they ask, they'll mail you a check for the amount of the loan. You must pay the annual interest expense on the loan, so that your policy stays in force under its original terms. If you don't pay the interest, they will either deduct it from your next dividend payment, or deduct it from your cash value. One way or the other, it has to be paid.

Advances on inheritance.   If you know you'll be inheriting money from an elderly parent or relative, you might ask them to advance you part of the money now. If they give you an annual gift of up to $10,000, they will not have to pay any taxes. This may be a way to reduce the overall estate taxes for the elderly relative, while giving you the cash you can put to use right away. Of course, you could receive more than $10,000, but the donor would be subject to gift and income tax assessments.

As these examples demonstrate, money to fund your business may be hiding in places that you haven't considered before. Your personal financial situation may present numerous other options to extract cash. Be creative and investigate many different options. The money you need may be closer than you think.

Chapter 9

Pulling Even Tighter on Your Bootstraps

Have you tapped into every imaginable financial asset and resource you can think of—and you still need cash? Does it seem like you're squeezing the proverbial blood from a turnip? If so, it's time to consider some serious bootstrapping ideas.

Get a part-time job. Don't groan and say you don't have time. If you really need money, get a part-time job—preferably during business downtime so it won't be a problem being away from the business. Also, find a job where you don't have to think too much. Remember, the purpose of this job isn't to build a career, rather it's to give you some cash. If you go to a nontaxing job for four hours a night, it's a small price to pay to build your business.

Ask your significant other. If you just cannot find your way into a tolerable part-time job, ask your significant other to get one. Now, the mere act of imagining this will make you think twice about your ability to do it yourself, so don't even ask until you are absolutely sure there is no other way. This is asking a lot of another person, but you'll know if you can make the request. Many businesses have struggled through growing pains while a sympathetic spouse took a less-than-optimal job to support the household during a rocky financial phase.

The bank of spouse. Another approach is to ask your spouse for a loan, or to be the cosigner on a bank loan. You may have decided to keep your financial lives separate—which can be a good risk-management strategy when you're building a business—and until now, you've never asked your spouse for a dime. But now may be the time. The downside risk of this arrangement is that your spouse's savings and personal credit may be the safety net beneath both of you, and your borrowing may weaken that secure backup. Another downside risk is emotional—when tension arises between you, money issues are often among the first shrieks to be heard during a fight. Again, you will know the right thing to do.

Spouse's health insurance.   If your spouse has a job where he or she is covered for health insurance, get onto this plan. It will save you lots of money for health insurance while the business is getting off the ground. Consider these funds to be money in the bank until the business employs enough people to merit getting group health insurance coverage.

Downsize your lifestyle.   Are there ways you can cut back in your daily life? While your immediate reaction is probably "No way!," there really are things you can do. First, evaluate what you are paying for rent. You can always move into a smaller house or apartment where your expenses would be lower. If you own your home, you may even think about selling it and moving into a more modest abode until your business gets off the ground. Look in the real estate section of the paper to get an idea of market rents in different neighborhoods.

If you live in a city with good public transportation, do you need to hold onto your car? Owning a car is a necessity in the suburbs, but in a city, you can often make do without one. When you need a car for business, you can rent one on those specific occasions. Eliminating a car immediately gets rid of automobile insurance, a possible garage space, and paying for the ongoing maintenance and fuel. Plus, you will have the cash in hand from selling it.

What are your eating habits? We're not talking about the major food groups here, but if you're eating out in restaurants, eat in at home. If you go out for lunch, go to a deli instead—or brown-bag it. You'll be shocked to see how this adds up.

We aren't going to belabor the ways you can downsize your lifestyle. Just know that it's possible, and take a hard look at what you can sacrifice right now. Often we're in the habit of living the lifestyle we had when we were earning our highest income, so there's probably some room for adjustment. If you're growling as you read this, perhaps it will be additional incentive to get your business to the next level so you won't need to employ these tactics.

Sale of collectibles.   Do you have any antiques, paintings, or other collectibles that you can sell? Since there is not a free and open market for this type of sale, you will need to see what outlets exist in your community. Check the classified section of your local paper, where you may come across someone who is interested in the kinds of things you are selling. Alternatively, you can place an ad in the paper offering your assets for sale.

Garage sales.   What an opportunity to clean out all the junk in your house! Garage sales are very popular and have been elevated to almost an art form in some communities. Find out where to advertise your sale (a classified in the local paper is a safe bet), and make sure you run the ad far enough in advance so people will know about your sale.

Be very organized on the big day. Buy a package of small labels and stick them on each item, along with your asking price. This way, you know in advance what you are charging and do not have to invent a price when a customer asks you. You might want to ask a friend or other family member to be with you on the day of the sale. The garage sale pros seem to come in big waves, and by having another person around, you can make more sales when many customers appear at once. Keep in mind that the garage sale pros come earlier than the designated time, so be ready an hour earlier than your stated beginning time.

Pawnbrokers.   This may seem like a low-brow option, but the pawn business is actually a legitimate, growing industry that is alive and well in this country. Some shops buy items outright; others offer loans at high interest rates. If you need the cash, forget your pride. Bring in an asset you can live without for awhile, get a loan, and use the proceeds for your business. (The pawnbroker won't sell the item being held as collateral as long as you're making payments. If you miss a payment, however, that treasured heirloom will be up for sale and you could lose it forever.) Or, sell a valuable to the pawnbroker outright and get the money you need instantly. Pawnbrokers are more popular in some areas of the country than others, and each state regulates them differently. If you're looking for cash in a hurry, review your possessions and look in the Yellow Pages for a pawnbroker near you.

Stay hopeful.   A desperate person can be spotted miles away, so don't put yourself in the position of being shark bait. Don't gamble to make more money; you will most certainly lose just because you are desperate for cash. In the same line, don't get involved with loan sharks. Instead, do a personal budget overhaul and review your expenses line by line to identify opportunities to save cash. There are often more places than you think where you can squeeze out some extra cash for your business.

Chapter 10

The World of Commercial Banks

The banking industry is undergoing significant restructuring these days. Big banks are merging to create larger financial institutions, and smaller banks are becoming more specialized in their communities. In choosing a bank, you need to consider the many different services you'll be needing in the next few years. As a small business, it is almost always better to centralize your banking activity with one bank, rather than spreading the business among two or more banks.

Banking services. When we think of banks, the image of tellers and checking accounts and loans comes to mind. But today's banks provide many more services, depending on their size and market focus. Will your business need to take MasterCard and Visa? These are merchant account services, made available by many of the larger banks. Will you be exporting any products? Banks can provide letters of credit and foreign exchange services to support your international business. Does your business collect money by mail from all over the country? Your bank can provide cash management services, such as lock boxes, which are centralized cash-collection points.

Think about what you are going to need down the road, and factor those ideas into your decision.

Eligibility for loans. There are many variables that go into a bank's decision to lend you money. In Chapter 28 you'll learn how bankable you are and in Chapter 31 you'll discover what the bank is looking for. For now, we'll assume that your company is eligible and discuss some of the available lending alternatives.

Short-Term Credit Facilities

To banks, *short-term* means less than one year, and these funds are extended to businesses to pay salaries, suppliers, and other day-to-day business needs while awaiting payment from customers. These are also referred to as *working capital loans.*

Line of credit.   This is a credit facility made available for a one-year period. You can borrow up to the designated limit and repay as you wish during the course of the year. Let's say you have just completed a big project for a customer, but you have not yet received payment. In the meantime, however, you need to pay your staff, so you would borrow the amount you need under the line of credit and repay it when you get paid by your customer.

How a line of credit works.   When talking about credit lines, there are some distinctions to keep in mind. The amount *available* under a line of credit is the maximum amount you can borrow at any time. What you actually borrow under that line is the *outstanding* amount, or *loan* amount. So, if the bank grants you a $50,000 line of credit, $50,000 is the maximum amount that you can borrow. If you draw down $10,000 under this line, that means that you have a loan of $10,000 or that $10,000 is *outstanding* under the line. In this example, you would be able to borrow up to $40,000 more.

Each bank operates a little differently, but when you borrow under the lines, each amount will be documented by a note (essentially an IOU). Interest will be due every 30, 60, or 90 days. Under this type of line, bankers expect what is called a *cleanup* month one time during the year, where you are paid up in full and have nothing outstanding under the line. By the way, sometimes this cleanup month occurs when it's least convenient for your company. Talk to your banker ahead of time so there are no surprises.

The purpose behind the cleanup is to prove that your need is for working capital, as opposed to more permanent capital. Ask your banker about this cleanup provision. When the one-year period comes to an end, it is time to discuss *renewing* the line of credit with your banker. The bank will review your financial statements for the year and make the decision based on your financial figures as well as your history as a borrower. Assuming there are no surprises, your line of credit should be renewed for another year.

An *unsecured* (no collateral pledged) line of credit is usually documented by a simple letter of agreement where the bank agrees to make funds available up to a certain amount at a particular interest rate. Most interest rates are based on the prime rate, which is the rate at which the largest banks lend money to corporate customers. You can find the prime rate in the *Wall Street Journal* or in the business section of your local paper. If the line of credit is *secured,* there is more documentation that would pertain to the collateral.

Variations on lines of credit.   Some banks make available *overdraft* lines to your checking account. This means that if you overdraw the account, the bank will automatically make a loan up to the approved amount. Overdraft lines are not intended to be used for general funding purposes; instead, they are to protect you from occasional bounced checks. They are expected to be repaid in a short period of time.

Longer-Term Credit Facilities

Banks may classify medium-term (one- to three-year) and long-term (four- to seven-year) loan periods, or they may just call anything over a year a *term loan*. Term loans are designed to finance capital needs that do not pay for themselves in a short period of time. The purchase of equipment, for example, can be financed by a term loan. In almost all cases, any term borrowings by small businesses need to be secured by collateral. While banks may be comfortable lending for working capital purposes, they are more wary of extending the time horizon when you're still building your business. Let's take a look at some examples of term facilities that may be offered by banks.

Installment loans. These are loans made for the purchase of equipment, for example, and have a fixed repayment schedule over a three- to five-year time period. The loan will be secured by the equipment, a fixed interest rate will be applied, and you will pay equal amounts on a monthly basis over the designated time period. If you've ever borrowed to buy a car, you've probably experienced an installment loan. The alternative to buying equipment and financing its purchase is to lease the equipment, which we'll discuss in Chapter 12.

Revolving credit/term loan. These are lines that allow the company to borrow and repay (similar to a line of credit) over a two- to three-year period. At the end of that time, whatever is outstanding converts to a term loan and is repaid on a monthly or quarterly basis over the next three to four years. While the mechanics may be similar to straight lines of credit, the difference is that you will be operating under a loan agreement, where you will need to comply with a number of financial covenants (requirements) each quarter. If you violate the loan agreement, the bank may call the loan, and you will have to repay everything immediately.

You need to have established a good track record before a bank will make this type of loan available, since the bank is projecting that you can manage credit over a longer time period. It's why these loans are a popular credit option for companies that are more established. They are usually made available when a company is undergoing a lot of growth and its working capital needs have accelerated dramatically.

The Approval Process

To obtain any of the credit facilities we've mentioned so far, you first need to prepare a credit application. In addition, the bank will ask for your company's financial statements (usually for the past three years), a list of accounts payable (amounts owed to your suppliers and vendors) and accounts receivable (amounts due to you from your customers), a detailed cash-flow statement, real estate appraisals (if appropriate), and any other documentation relevant to your situation. In addition, you may be asked to present your personal tax returns, especially if you are asked to guarantee the loan.

Credit scoring.   This is a mathematical model that statistically analyzes a business's financial condition and the owner's personal credit. The resulting score is used to decide whether you should be granted credit. Credit scoring came about as a way to systematize lending to small businesses.

The process serves to weed out companies that are not creditworthy and to approve those that are good credit risks. Many companies fall into the gray area in the middle; in those cases, a bank representative will evaluate the company's application personally. The thing to remember is that the larger banks are not necessarily going to give you any time. They may be happy to lend you money—if you are creditworthy, that is—but they do not have time to devote to getting to know you as well as a community bank officer would. Some of the smaller banks use credit scoring as well, but your loan application will likely be reviewed by a loan officer.

This is one of the trade-offs you need to consider when deciding between large versus small banks. As a small company, you may get lost in the shuffle of a large bank. But larger banks can provide many benefits as your business grows. Banks are in business to make money, and the reality is that the return from small business loans and fees from checking accounts do not usually constitute a profitable piece of business for the larger banks. Things like credit scoring have actually helped small businesses by creating a systematic way to evaluate small business loans. The process has reduced the labor-intensive aspects of credit review, and banks can review a greater number of applications.

The "traditional" approach.   While the mathematical approach of credit scoring is used by many banks, both large and small, a traditional review of your company evaluates the same types of things. Banks want you to have been in business for two to three years. They will initially want to secure everything to protect themselves. For example, they may take a lien on your assets (a collateral pledge on what you own) and ask for your personal guarantee. If the company's debt-to-equity ratio is greater than 3 to 1 (meaning you're carrying too much debt; explained further in Chapter 38), they'll probably turn you down and refer you to a finance company. Banks always expect to be paid back through the cash flow of the business, and they also look to a secondary source of repayment (for example, selling off the assets you've pledged as collateral).

Where to find banks.   If you don't have a business banking relationship and don't know where to turn, talk to other business owners in your network for referrals, or ask for help from your local chamber of commerce. If you're given a specific loan officer's name, call and make an appointment. If you don't have a name, it might be worthwhile to just show up at the designated branch where you would want to do business, and ask to speak to the branch manager. That person will then direct you to someone who will look after your business.

Make sure that your loan is housed in a branch or service center that handles other businesses of the same size. You don't want your company to get lost in the shuffle because it is a fraction of the size of other firms. Also, cultivate relationships with more than one person at your bank. If your main contact leaves and it is time to renew your line of credit, the new loan officer will be starting from scratch and won't have history with you.

A small manufacturing company we know faced this situation when it needed to borrow from its local bank for a production run. The line of credit was about to expire and the bank officer who originally signed the credit line had been transferred to a larger branch. The new loan officer was reluctant to automatically renew the line because he was unfamiliar with the company. Fortunately, this small business owner had all of the proper documentation ready to present to the bank, immediately made an appointment to see the banker, and was able to seamlessly borrow to pay for the production cycle.

There are a number of other financial institutions that walk and talk and act like commercial banks, but are not. In Figure 10.1, we've outlined some of these other nonbank lending institutions.

Figure 10.1

THE NONBANK BANKS

Thrifts Savings & loan institutions	Traditionally real estate lenders; now doing more commercial lending
Credit unions	Increasingly available; offer many of the consumer banking services of commercial banks
Brokerage firms	Larger ones are creating full-service loan and depository services for small business customers
Credit card companies	Setting up full-service small business divisions
Commercial finance companies	Traditionally asset-based lenders; now increasing commercial lending

Chapter 11

Understanding Asset-Based Lending

If your overall financial picture is jittery, but you have great customers, asset-based lending may be a good option for obtaining money for your business. Asset-based lending is used when you have high-quality assets—receivables, inventory, or equipment—you can pledge as collateral for a loan. It is a frequently used funding alternative for many small business owners, particularly those who may otherwise be turned down for bank loans. The good news is that your company may not be *bankable,* but it is *financeable.* That is, the bank may not want to give you money, but there are other financial institutions that will.

Nature of these assets. *Accounts receivable* (sometimes called *receivables*) are the uncollected portion of sales you have made. For instance, if you sold $10,000 of product to a client on 30-day terms, it means that the customer will pay you $10,000 within 30 days. During the time between the actual delivery of the product and the receipt of the $10,000, this sale is actually an account receivable, a short-term asset on your company's balance sheet. When you get paid, the receivable disappears, and you receive cash.

Inventory, product you hold for resale, is divided into three components: raw materials, work in process, and finished goods. There is a value placed on each of these components, depending on the actual goods and the marketability of the inventory. *Equipment* can be anything from a printing press to a building to a computer network. Equipment is less frequently financed by asset-based lenders, but it is eligible collateral. Some asset-based lenders also will advance your firm money against *purchase orders,* which are unfilled customer orders.

How it works. As an example, Azur Packaging Company is a box manufacturer that sells specialized packaging to pharmaceutical companies. It has $125,000 in receivables from various customers and needs to pay its paper supplier faster than it receives payment from the pharmaceutical customers. Azur goes to a commercial finance company and receives a loan pledged by those receivables as collateral. In essence, Azur is saying, "We have $125,000 coming in a month from now, but we need the money immediately to pay our suppliers. Give us a loan, and you'll be repaid as soon as we get paid."

Who are the lenders? You will sometimes find asset-based lenders in banks, but commercial finance companies and credit companies specialize in this kind of lending. Two well-known firms are GE Capital and The Money Store. In contrast to banks, these lenders are not as concerned about your company's profits, net worth, or debt burden. Instead, they collateralize high-quality assets, such as receivables or inventory, and make loans against them. While the loans are granted based strictly on the quality of the collateral, they're looking for repayment from your company first, not a selling off of your collateral if you don't make good on the loan. They're making assumptions of timely payment and good credit on the part of your customers.

Terms of the loans. Asset-based loans can be made as short-term loans secured by the receivables. These loans are virtually always more expensive than traditional bank loans. Why? Because your credit quality isn't as high, even though you have valuable collateral. Interest rates on these types of loan average at prime plus 3 to 5 percent, plus an origination fee of about 1 to 2 percent. We agree that it's steep, but keep in mind the benefits the much-needed cash will bring your company.

The loans are typically made against receivables that are less than 60 days old—ones that are less risky and have a higher probability of being paid. When you receive payment for the receivable, you pay the lender and that portion of your loan outstanding is paid down.

Asset-based loans are made against *eligible* assets, meaning those that are not past due or are of risky credit quality. There are different *advance rates* applied, depending on the collateral. Some rules of thumb are:

✓ 75 to 80 percent advance against eligible receivables
✓ 25 to 50 percent advance against eligible inventory
✓ 10 to 50 percent advance against equipment
✓ Up to 75 percent against real estate

For example, Azur Packaging Company has $115,000 in eligible receivables; the other $10,000 are not eligible because they are 90 days past due. The finance company lends Azur $86,250, which represents a 75-percent advance against the $115,000 in eligible receivables.

When this lending makes sense.   We recommend that you always first try to get a traditional bank loan, primarily because the interest rates will be much more favorable. If you're turned down because of shaky credit quality, ask your banker for referrals to asset-based lenders. Your bank may have a department that does this type of lending, or they may refer you to finance companies that specialize in asset-based lending. Asset-based lenders are much less likely to turn you away if your overall financial situation is shaky, and they'll take you if the quality of your collateral—the receivables, inventory, or equipment—is good.

Factors.   These are lenders who actually purchase your receivables at a discount and advance you about 80 percent of the discounted value in cash. Factors bear both the collection and credit risks of payment. For example, you may have $275,000 of receivables, which the factor discounts to $250,000. The factoring firm will purchase those receivables for $200,000 (80-percent advance rate in this case) and pay your company in cash. The factor then takes care of the bookkeeping and collections, and assumes all the losses on the uncollectible accounts— making their profit for taking the risk and providing these services to you.

Advance rates (the percentage of your receivables the factor gives you in cash) have a huge range, and may be anywhere from 70 to 95 percent of the value of the receivables. Factors' pricing is based on your sales volume, the average invoice size, the number of customers, the credit quality of your customers, and the terms of sale. For budgeting purposes, assume that you will be paying prime plus 5 percent, plus around 1 percent on the total volume for collections and insurance.

If you've had experience with companies in the apparel and textile industries, then you've probably encountered factors. Companies in these fields are frequent customers of factors, since their receivables are their key assets. For example, let's say you're a clothing manufacturer selling to department stores and independent boutiques. You've shipped your product to the stores on terms of net 30 (meaning you'll be paid in 30 days). If you need cash right away, think about selling these receivables to a factor. The factoring firm will do a check on each of your customers and make you an offer based on their creditworthiness. The trade-off is that you'll end up with less money than if you had waited for each of your customers to pay, but you'll have funds you can put to work immediately in your business.

Companies often start out with factors or other asset-based lenders because their traditional banking options appear limited. Once their overall credit quality improves, they inevitably move on to traditional banks, since the costs associated with asset-based lending is so much higher. As a result, there is a lot of turnover among the customers of these lenders.

How to prepare.   When you approach an asset-based lender, have all of your documentation in place: invoices, shipping records, advance payments, and so forth. Once you become a client of an asset-based lender, expect frequent meetings—usually monthly—going over all of your records. These lenders do not like surprises, so they keep on top of your finances (translation: *you!*) as long as you have their money.

When you're shopping around for a lender, call and ask for the officer who handles small business accounts. Introduce yourself and describe what you're looking for. Be prepared to answer questions about the type of customers you have, and the average size of the receivable. Assuming the information you give them fits with their client profile, the next step will be to arrange an in-person meeting.

Where to find asset-based lenders and factors.   Again, ask your banker for a referral. You may also try your accountant and the local chamber of commerce for suggestions. If you're in a position to choose, interview three or four asset-based lenders and factors before making your decision. Make sure you are comparing apples to apples as it pertains to pricing and services. You may also call the Commercial Finance Association at (212) 594-3490, or check its Web site at http://www.cfonline.com/cfa.htm for a membership list. Finally, you can look under *factors* or *finance companies* in your local Yellow Pages.

Understand that working with a finance company or factor, while more expensive than a bank, may be the only way you fund the growth of your company. Think of it as a rite of passage, and know that it is money well spent to move your business to the next level.

Chapter 12

Leasing Options

L easing is a convenient way to finance expensive purchases without spending a lot of cash up front. For most companies, there are two general categories of items commonly leased: equipment and commercial office space. In this chapter, we take a look at both of them.

Equipment Leasing

How does leasing work? The lender, called the *lessor,* actually owns the equipment and rents it to your company, the *lessee,* under specified terms over a period of time. You can often finance 100 percent of the cost of the equipment, as opposed to paying a down payment up front—a big benefit to cash-strapped companies. As the lessee, you do not own the equipment (so you have no asset to record), and do not have any liability (loan) recorded on your books either. This is an advantage because your company doesn't have the additional debt burden that comes from having a traditional loan.

You can also deduct lease payments as operating expenses, just as you would deduct interest expense. Another benefit is that your company doesn't get stuck owning equipment that becomes obsolete in a relatively short time, such as computer systems.

This type of financing is a natural for companies that use equipment to manufacture their product, but there are many other applications as well, such as leasing computer or telecommunications equipment. Leasing is an excellent option for growing businesses, since you only need to pay a monthly lease expense instead of incurring the all-at-once expense hit of purchasing high-priced equipment.

What kind of equipment can be leased? Virtually any kind of equipment, new or used, can be leased. Automobiles, heavy equipment, telecommunications systems, computers, and electronic equipment are but a few examples. If your business needs cars for the salespeople, fleet leasing is an option. If you need to upgrade your telephone system, leasing is a way to do it with virtually no cash down.

Why not just buy the equipment?   You can. In fact, there may be situations where it is more advantageous to buy the equipment and borrow against it. In that situation, you'd take out a loan to buy the equipment, invest a down payment, and use the equipment as collateral. You'd end up with a new asset on your balance sheet (the equipment) and also a new liability (the loan). You would own the equipment, maintain it, insure it, and take the risk of obsolescence. Over time, it may cost you more to lease than to buy the equipment outright, so you need to evaluate leasing versus borrowing to purchase the equipment on a case-by-case basis.

Lease agreements.   Treat a leasing agreement the same way you would a loan agreement. Know all of the details—including what the monthly payments will be, any hidden costs, what your responsibilities are as lessee (for example, are you responsible for insurance?), and so forth. Review the lease agreement with an attorney just to make sure that you're properly covered.

Who is in the leasing business?   Banks are in this business, as well as specialized leasing companies. First ask your banker for referrals; if your bank doesn't do leasing, your banker will be able to send you to a specialist. Your chamber of commerce is another resource, as is the Yellow Pages. Check listings under *leasing,* and make sure you specifically ask the type of leasing the firm does (equipment versus cars, for example).

For more information on leasing, contact the Equipment Leasing Association of America. They can be reached at (703) 527-8655 or via their Internet Web site at http://www.elaonline.com/elaadres.htm.

Commercial Leasing

When it comes time to rent a commercial space for your business, you'll enter the world of commercial leasing. Your ability to strike a good deal can pay off in cash-flow savings for years to come. Here are some tips to consider:

    ✓   Don't incur a commercial lease until you have to. The additional overhead is something that will stay with you for a long time. Nonetheless, at some point, your company will need more space.

✓ Understand how rent is calculated and what will trigger a rent increase.

✓ Shop around and look at different properties in different areas of town. Sometimes a few blocks can make a big difference in price. Even being on a side street instead of a main avenue can dramatically affect your costs.

✓ Evaluate what property and casualty insurance requirements the lease requires, and determine what is truly necessary and what is superfluous. Both your lawyer and insurance broker can help here.

✓ Leasehold improvements are a great way to save money. This is construction work that needs to be done on your leased space to make it work for your business. Depending on the cycle in the market, you may be able to negotiate for your landlord to absorb most, if not all, of these leasehold improvements. This can be thousands of dollars of savings if properly negotiated.

✓ Take a lease term that is sensible—not too long and not too short. Don't worry about outgrowing the space too early in the lease term; usually landlords are willing to relocate you to a larger space (which, of course, means more income to them).

✓ Your company is the obligor on the lease, and sometimes you will be asked to personally guarantee the lease. Try to avoid this wherever possible, because you will be personally liable if for some reason you need to break the lease before the term expires.

✓ Make sure you negotiate the right to sublet your commercial space. The landlords don't like this, especially in a market where rents are rising. They don't want you to be renting out the space and making a profit. By having the right to sublet, you protect yourself in the event that you cannot continue to rent the space.

Most commercial leases are standard contracts with pages of boilerplate clauses. The leasing agent will tell you that everything is standard, and just sign. That is obviously advice favoring the landlord—*always* read all the small print, and have an attorney review the lease to make sure there is nothing that will come back to haunt you.

For example, one business owner we know found an obscure clause in her lease pertaining to her company's responsibility to maintain the sprinkler system for fire safety. In examining the space, she couldn't even *see* a sprinkler system. It turned out that the sprinkler system was hidden by a dropped ceiling—and it had not been installed according to building code. If the sprinklers were set off, the ceiling would have caved in completely, and her company would have been liable for the damages. By catching this in advance, the reconfiguration of the sprinklers and bringing the ceiling up to code became preconditions for her signing the lease.

Both equipment leasing and commercial leasing are situations where your company is in effect renting someone else's property—equipment, in the case of operating leases, and real estate, in the case of commercial leases. Leasing can offer big benefits to companies that need to make expensive investments but are tight on cash. Evaluate your options and see if leasing makes sense—and be sure to pay attention to the fine print and have an attorney cast an eye over the paperwork.

Chapter 13

Strategic Alliances and Partnerships

While you may be strongly marching down the path of managing and growing your businesses as a solo business owner, there may come a time when a strategic alliance or partnership makes sense for your business. By engaging in such a venture, you'll be bringing some combination of financing and management expertise to your company. Whatever the reason, there are a number of factors to consider in making such a decision.

A *partnership* is a legal entity where two or more people share the risk and the rewards of an enterprise. A *strategic alliance* is an arrangement between two companies that combine resources to gain additional business. Some strategic alliances are formal written agreements; others are informal as a handshake. Some involve a sharing of resources and an exchange of funds; others are as simple as a cooperative marketing arrangement. Whatever their structure, one goal prevails: strategic alliances are opportunities for small businesses to accomplish things that would otherwise take much more money and/or staff time.

The "Lone Ranger." At this point in your company's development, you may be struggling with the business and sorely tempted by the thought of sharing your sorrows and joys with a partner. One of the major issues of running a business is the isolation that exists as you build the company and are unable to afford a large staff. While the appeal of a partner can be great, think about your management style and personality: Will you be able to share the spotlight with a partner? How comfortable will you be when you relinquish control to another person—especially if you have put all your energy and dreams into the project until now? Can you share your vision to the extent that you give up part of it to a partner?

Unless you start a business from the beginning with another person, it's often difficult to shift into a partnership midstream. If two or more people have an idea, bring complimentary strengths to the venture, create a solid plan, and are all passionately driven to make it work, then a partnership has a good chance of succeeding. They all share the vision from the beginning, and that is a key element of their collective strength.

These concerns about giving up control and the risk of finding appropriate partners are just two of the challenges facing entrepreneurs as they build their companies. Fortunately, there are several ways you can partner with another person or company to bring money and/or expertise into your business.

In creating a strategic alliance, as with any alliance, remember that communication is key. Be honest about what you seek to gain, and look for situations that are win/win for both parties. The variations on these alliances are unlimited; here are a few of the more common ones we've seen work best:

Partner with a key customer. Perhaps your company sells a substantial amount of product to one large corporation. If so, you have an opportunity to form a strategic alliance, especially if the product is in high demand by this company. It's risky enough if one customer represents more than 10 percent of your sales; if any customer buys a third or half of your product, it could make sense to arrange a long-term alliance to assure the continuation of the relationship. The contract will reduce your risk and may provide the foundation for expanding into other business lines.

Partner with your former employer. Many entrepreneurs jump-start their new companies by having a strong relationship with a former employer. For example, you may develop a product or service that provides your employer with a solution to a major problem. You make arrangements to go into your own business selling this product or service, and your former employer offers you a long-term contract with his or her company. The bonus: You end up with great cash flow, and the long-term contract with a creditworthy company means you can go to other lenders and possibly get other financing you need.

Partner with a competitor. No, that's not a misprint. Successful entrepreneurs always know who their best competitors are. It's important to stay in touch with the goings-on of your competition for many reasons. One you may not have thought of, however, is to engage them if you secure a contract for something larger than your company can handle on its own. When hiring permanent staff is not a financially viable option, this is an excellent economic and strategic solution.

This approach works particularly well with service businesses. You may have a growing graphic design business, for example, and have landed a contract three times larger than any previous one. You know you can't make the deadline with your current staff, but if you have relationships with some of your best competitors, you can contract them for the project. The key is to cultivate these relationships where appropriate. One of the happy consequences of hiring a competitor is that they may enlist your company's assistance in a similar situation in the future.

Partner for cross marketing.   This strategy is for two distinct businesses to collectively market to a target customer base. Both companies pool their resources and have greater marketing impact than if they prospected individually. And, of course, they both save money in the process. An example might be a videographer and a communications consultant who want to produce industrial films with pharmaceutical companies. The videographer has expertise in medical photography and the communications consultant is a health care specialist. Together they can market their businesses, with the expectation of teaming together on projects.

There are many other situations where alliances make sense. Whatever alliance you may enter into, keep these points in mind:

✓ Even though your companies may be small, tread carefully around sharing information related to fees. You don't want to find your company accused of price fixing.

✓ When cultivating relationships with large corporations, make sure that you have connections with several people in the company. Think of what would happen if your sole contact left—your company might be dropped at the next contract negotiation.

✓ Be creative when exploring alliances—there will certainly be opportunities where your unique business is a natural partner for a strategic venture.

✓ When in doubt, consult your attorney and CPA about any gray areas of your strategic relationship.

✓ Keep the end in mind: You are partnering with another company to expand your business and to increase your cash flow by pooling financial and managerial resources.

Another option to strategic alliances is to consider partnerships with individuals who would become employees. Here's one of the most successful arrangements we've seen for growing companies:

Hire a key employee with ownership incentive.   This strategy involves bringing in a strong manager in a critical area that needs specific expertise. It could be marketing, sales, manufacturing—whatever needs beefing up. You may have comfort in this person being an equal partner in your company, but you really need his or her expertise.

The solution is to offer a relatively low base salary with upside potential in the form of stock ownership, which would vest (become fully owned and controlled by the employee) over time. The lower salary is the equivalent of an interest-free loan, because you are paying *less* than market rate for a manager. The sort of person who would accept a lower salary with the upside potential is someone who will work hard to make that stock ownership not just a reality, but high value—in essence, someone who wants the company to be as successful as you do.

Your company may have started out as a solo enterprise, and you still want it to remain that way—but you see the value in making connections. Or, your business has now grown to include one or more employees and you're looking for ways to expand your reach without generating a lot of debt or overhead. For these situations, and many more, strategic alliances and partnerships are a smart solution. Design them any way you want—keeping in mind a win/win philosophy—and you'll discover ways to grow your business without the direct use of money.

Chapter 14

The Power of Angels

W hen we speak of angels in a book on business finance, we don't mean the type with wings. (Although to many entrepreneurs, these angels do have halos!) In a business context, angels are wealthy private investors, typically entrepreneurs, who have an interest in supporting businesses in startup or expansion mode. Like friends and family, they are placing their bets on you—but that's where the similarity ends. These folks give you money, expect a high financial return on their investment, and also pass along their expertise.

Angel motivation. The prototypical angel is a wealthy individual, close to or in retirement, who is looking for a way to diversify his or her investment portfolio. Angels seek companies in which they can make a better return than in alternative investments, such as stocks, bonds, or other securities. In exchange for their money, angels will either take seats on the board of directors or take an active managerial voice in the major decisions of your company. One of the great benefits for the entrepreneur who uses angel financing is the informal mentoring he or she receives from the investor.

Angel investments range from as little as a few thousand dollars to $1 million, and they virtually always invest in businesses they understand. Since these investments are always risky, they usually moderate their risk by investing in businesses or industries in which they have first-hand experience. They understand the general risks involved with giving seed money to an unproven venture, but they're not giving it away as they would to a charity. They expect a rate of return that makes it worthwhile to park their money outside of more traditional investment options. For example, a 20-percent annual return is a good place to begin discussions with an angel.

Be prepared: Angel investors are going to scrutinize your passion, your skills, your commitment, and your character. Don't talk to an angel unless you are 110-percent passionate about your company, and you can demonstrate that you've put your own personal assets into the business. Angels will want you to prove your-self worthy of the investment on all levels. Your ability to articulate your vision is paramount in this process—you want this investor to see your company's future as clearly as you do. If you can do this, the investor will be more likely to buy into your product or concept, and will also see the reality of receiving his or her invest-ment back after a number of years.

Where to find them.   Private investors can be found everywhere—you just need to start paying attention. CEOs or executive managers of large companies in your industry are great resources. They may have an interest in investing them-selves, and alternatively, they will have an extensive network of friends and asso-ciates. You can find these people either through your own personal network, or by making connections at industry conferences and conventions. Most angels live within a day's drive of their investments, so they can be close by for consultation.

Other investors can be found in professional services: Attorneys and CPAs are great resources because they will have an extensive client base. You'll find that many partners in these law and accounting firms are also interested in investing themselves. Here again, familiarity is important. They may have an interest in investing in a business in which they have had experience.

Watch for conflict of interest, though. Don't ask your CPA to invest in your business, for example, and expect him or her to maintain the relationship as your accountant. The accounting function is by nature an arm's length relationship—how valid could your company's financial statements be if your CPA was a major investor? Take care to maintain high ethical standards, as you would expect from your clients or associates.

Networks.   Sometimes angel investors pool their resources and invest in a variety of businesses that are seeking either startup or expansion capital. You can find networks that invest in specific industries, regional companies, women- or minority-owned businesses, and others.

The Angel Capital Electronic Network, ACE-*Net,* is sponsored by the SBA's Office of Advocacy. It was established in October 1996 to use the technology of the Internet to bring together small businesses seeking capital and the investment community. The intent is for ACE-*Net* to become a private, independent not-for-profit organization after it is operating for awhile.

ACE-*Net* is for investors who want to raise between $250,000 and $5 mil-lion—resources that are beyond most friends and families, yet are too small for most venture capitalists. Entrepreneurs complete a Small Corporate Offering Reg-istration (SCOR) application and pay an annual subscription fee of $450. Your company will then be part of the database of available investments. Interested investors scan the database looking for investments that meet their specific crite-ria and directly contact the companies seeking capital. Check out the ACE-*Net* Web site at http://ace-net.sr.unh.edu for further information.

The following is a listing of the ACE-*Net* founding members and their specific Web sites:

- ✓ Bay Area Regional Technology Alliance
  http://www.barta.org
- ✓ Ben Franklin Technology Center
  http://www.benfranklin.org
- ✓ Kansas Technology Enterprise Corporation
  http://www.ktech.com
- ✓ MERRA
  http://www.merra.com
- ✓ Office of Advocacy of the U.S. Small Business Administration
  http://www.sba.gov/ADVO
- ✓ The Capital Network
  http://www.thecapitalnetwork.com
- ✓ UCSD Connect
  http://darwin1.ucsd.edu:8000/connect
- ✓ Whittemore School of Business and Economics, University of New Hampshire
  http://www.unh.edu/wsbe

Other angel resources.   Another Internet resource is the Capital Match-maker, which features companies seeking a minimum of $25,000 of capital. The cost of listing your financing requirement is scaled according to how much money you want to raise. For further information, visit the Web site at http://www.matchmaker.org/capital.

Some of the world's greatest technology firms, including Hewlett-Packard and Apple Computer, had their beginnings in California garages. That innovative spirit is the inspiration for garage.com, an Internet-based company dedicated to helping entrepreneurs and investors build high-tech businesses. Acting as an online matchmaker, garage.com offers assistance to entrepreneurs seeking seed level financing as well as advice, mentoring, and research help. For investors, the service presents prescreened financial opportunities that match an investor's identified interests, in a format that helps them evaluate companies quickly and easily. For more information, visit the Web site at http://www.garage.com.

While these angel networks provide a vast pool of capital to small business owners, remember that your own Rolodex can be just as valuable to you. Your existing personal connections can provide you with a number of introductions to local business executives who already know you within your local business community. It's certainly helpful to research angels wherever they may be, but don't forget your own back yard!

Chapter 15

The High Stakes of Venture Capital

T he expression *venture capital* evokes both excitement and mystique in the eyes of entrepreneurs who want to raise money—*big* money. We realize that most readers of this book may be years away from this type of financing or may never desire it at all. It's important to understand this level of financing, however, because it can stretch your mind into thinking of new opportunities for your business.

Venture capitalists (VCs) are individuals or firms that seek extraordinary returns in high-growth companies. In exchange for their investment, they often take a controlling position in the company. This control extends from having several seats on the board of directors to having a voice in the strategic and tactical decisions that a company makes.

How they invest. Venture capitalists often make equity investments in companies. This means that they are owners, and that they expect a high appreciation in the equity (stock) over a period of time. They will also lend money in high-yielding loans and often offer hybrid securities (a combination of debt and equity), such as convertible debt (a high-yielding loan that converts to stock at a certain point in time) or preferred stock. This is sometimes referred to as *mezzanine financing*.

A **high-yielding loan** *is one that carries high interest rates to compensate for the greater level of risk in making the loan.*

Criteria. These investors are looking for investments in companies that have great ideas that can take off and make everyone a lot of money. These ideas are usually at the stage where there is some evidence of the market potential, and it is a matter of obtaining capital to launch the venture. A venture capitalist will never invest without having a clear idea of his or her exit strategy: how he or she will be able to cash out of the investment. The exit time frame is in the 5- to 10-year range, with an average of 7 years.

Prequalifications.   Generally speaking, venture capitalists want to see companies that are greater than $5 million in sales that need to raise $1 million or more. These companies should have three years of financial records. In addition to wanting out in seven years, venture capitalists look for a compound annualized rate of return of 30 to 35 percent. Not all venture capital investments are successful, which is why they have a high price attached to them. Your business or idea has to be in an industry that typically receives high returns. Popular venture-backed industries these days include technology, communications, biotechnology, and medical solutions, although nearly any industry has businesses with venture potential. As you can see, it's not the industry as much as the type of business; the typical mom-and-pop business is not the target of traditional venture capitalists.

How to approach.   If you think your business fits a venture capitalist's profile, call a few companies and ask if they are making any investments at this time. If they are, ask what types of investments they are looking for and the size of investment they make in companies. If your business seems to fit within this description and the investment amount fits, tell them about your business. They will tell you if they are interested in seeing a package.

Ask how they prefer to see packages, and *do what they say!* If they want it in a format that is different from your presentation, alter it before you submit it. Don't put yourself in a position where you are eliminated from consideration because you were too lazy or arrogant to repackage your proposal.

Things to consider.   Let's say you've found a venture capitalist who likes your idea and you're in the courting stages. Be aware that this can be like a shark feeding frenzy if you don't watch out. If you give up control, you may be giving up everything you have worked for. Control comes in different forms, so use an excellent attorney who has negotiated these kinds of deals before.

The most obvious challenge will be if they ask for 51 percent of the equity (ownership) of the business. This may seem like you are giving up control, but there are ways to structure it with voting stock, for example, to work around the control issue. Remember, your objective is to make your dream a reality. Venture capitalists want high returns on investment, and they will take over to reach *their* goals. You may be the inventor and visionary behind this great idea, while they think you are the worst person to manage and grow the business. If you have not adequately protected your interests in structuring your venture capital deal, you may find yourself on the outside and not even know what happened.

Special situations.   In addition to the traditional venture capitalists, there are specialized funds. Some can be sponsored by nonprofit organizations. Others are designated for special interest groups, such as women or minorities. The criteria for financial returns can be somewhat less rigorous in these cases, since one of the key objectives may be to make capital available to those who may not have as much access to growth capital.

How it happens.   To give you a better idea of how the venture capital pieces come together, let's take a look at a hypothetical situation involving a small business and venture capital. John is the owner of a medical research company. He is a medical doctor whose career has focused on biotech research. Having invested over $500,000 of his own money, he has come up with a genetic application on a microchip which, if successful, would be a scientific breakthrough for victims of neurological diseases.

John needs $2 million to create the prototype and receive FDA approval. A venture capital firm specializing in biotech companies likes John's proposal and is evaluating the risks of this investment. While they are dazzled with John's brilliance as a researcher, they are not as comfortable with his skills as a CEO. Assuming the product is approved, they want to put in their own person to run the business.

The venture capital investors soon hire an outside CEO and John stays on as chairman. While he's not running the business, he's doing what he does best—taking his research to the next level. John will likely make money down the road if a larger firm buys his company or his company goes public.

Where to find venture capitalists.   There are a variety of resources to locate venture capital investors. Some of the most popular include the following:

The International Venture Capital Institute (IVCI), (203) 323-3143
The IVCI publishes the following two directories:
- ✓ Directory of Venture Networking Organizations and Related Resources
- ✓ Directory of Seed and Early Stage Venture Funds in the United States

Pratt's Guide to Venture Capital Sources, (212) 765-5311

American Express Small Business, www.americanexpress.com/smallbusiness
The American Express Small Business Web site features two venture capital resources, presented on a state-by-state basis.
- ✓ Venture capital companies by state:
  http://www.aexp.com/smallbusiness/resources/expanding/vcco.shtml
- ✓ Venture capital clubs on a statewide basis:
  http://www.aexp.com/smallbusiness/resources/expanding/vccl

Capital Venture, http://www.capitalventure.com
Formed in 1994, this organization serves as a clearinghouse for information on venture capital. They host local events in Boston and Atlanta; their Web site features an extensive list of hotlinks to venture capital firms and information.

National Venture Capital Association (NVCA), (703) 524-2549, http://www.nvca.org
Membership in this association is comprised of over 200 professional venture capital organizations.

MIT Enterprise Forum, Inc., (818) 395-3916, http://www.caltech.edu/~entforum
MIT's Enterprise Forum serves technologically oriented companies. There are 18 chapters in the United States and overseas; the Caltech chapter serves high-tech ventures in Southern California.

New York Venture Group (NYVG), (212) 832-6984
This group holds a monthly forum in New York City, bringing together business owners, equity investors and lenders, and related business professionals.

Oklahoma Investment Forum, (918) 585-1201
An annual forum targeting start up companies seeking less than $1 million

The Great Midwest Venture Capital Conference, (317) 264-2820
Up to 30 presentations are made at each conference.

Pennsylvania Private Investors Group's Monthly Showcase, (610) 975-9430
A monthly investment forum.

Chapter 16

Small Business Investment Companies

*S*mall Business Investment Companies (SBICs) are venture capital firms that are licensed and regulated by the Small Business Administration. Think of these as venture capital alternatives for Main Street, USA. They are not looking for the same sky-high returns as traditional venture capitalists. Their mandate is to fund small companies that otherwise have limited access to capital.

Who are they? SBICs are partnerships between the private and public sector to finance capital growth of small businesses. They can be independent venture firms or can be wholly owned subsidiaries of commercial banks.

Commercial banks often invest in SBIC subsidiaries as a way to support small businesses and invest in more venture capital types of transactions. They use their own private capital as well as funds guaranteed by the SBA to provide financing to small businesses.

Specialized Small Business Investment Companies (SSBICs) are special interest SBICs that provide assistance to small businesses that are owned by socially or economically disadvantaged persons.

SBICs and SSBICs invest in a wide range of industries—from high-tech to medical, telecommunications to manufacturing, computer services to distribution companies. While they may seek businesses that make new products with high profit potential, they also look for strong businesses with good growth potential.

Their investments can be either straight equity or debt. The debt is often in the form of *subordinated debt,* which sometimes carries warrants. Think of subordinated debt as longer term than traditional debt. (Subordinated debt usually carries a higher interest rate because it's riskier to give a longer-term loan; it usually gets paid back *after* traditional long-term debt, which is why it's called *subordinated.*) Warrants are options to buy stock at a designated time in the future. This feature gives subordinated debt with warrants a hybrid nature—it is both debt and equity.

How to approach an SBIC.   This is similar to the previous discussions about angel financing or traditional venture capital. Call your local SBA office and ask for the *Directory of Operating Small Business Investment Companies.* This guide is updated annually and has a state-by-state listing of active SBICs and SSBICs. It will give you a good idea of what funding options are available and helpful information to know before you contact the firms. In addition to the usual contact information, it lists the sources of capital of each firm and their ownership and investment policies. You can find lists of SBICs on the SBA's Web site at www.sba.gov/inv. Alternatively, you may want to check out the SBA's online database, called Angel Capital Electronic Network (ACE-*Net*), referred to in Chapter 14.

A directory published by the National Association of Small Business Investment Companies (NASBIC) lists most of the active SBICs. It also contains information on accounting or law firms that work with entrepreneurs. Call NASBIC at (202) 628-5055 to ask for the directory ($25), or mail your check (payable to NASBIC) to NASBIC Directory, P.O. Box 2039, Merrifield, VA 22116.

Make your phone calls to the appropriate firms and see if they have money available for investment. When you are talking to them, identify whether this will be a good fit for your company. While many SBICs invest in many different businesses, some specialize in specific industries. In New York City, for example, a number of the SBICs specialize in medallion lending (lending to people who want to purchase New York City taxi medallions). Since the number of medallions—and, hence, the number of taxis—is restricted in New York City, the medallion has a high market value. Some of these SBICs and SSBICs have built their loan and investment portfolios around this very specialized expertise.

What to present.   The SBIC will want to see your completed business plan, company financial statements, and other financial documents. Include a cover page with your actual request for funds and an explanation of what you will do with the money. If you're looking for equity, the firm will want to know when it will be able to cash out, although the emphasis on exit strategy is not as significant as it is with traditional venture capitalists. Like any investor, the SBIC wants to know why your company is a good risk and what you have to offer as the owner/operator of the firm.

Eligibility.   Your company must meet the SBA's definition of *small business.* At the time of writing, *small* means a company with a net worth of $18 million or less, and average net income after taxes for the past 2 years of no greater than $6 million. The main objective is for SBICs to fund small businesses, not larger ones. SBICs can make long-term loans to small business companies that need money to expand and grow. The SBIC may work alone or in conjunction with a private lender. The loan maturity is no less than 5 years, and no greater than 20 years, providing a much longer term than traditional commercial lenders.

SBICs can also lend debt securities, such as subordinated debt or preferred stock, depending on the small business's needs. SBICs are also able to purchase equity in small businesses, but they cannot become a general partner in an unincorporated business.

When you become a customer of an SBIC, be prepared for a very close working relationship. The SBIC account team will provide you with management assistance as you grow your business. The downside of working with an SBIC is the cost—you'll be paying interest rates in the 14- to 19-percent range or higher. Nonetheless, this can be a good alternative when you have limited options and a long-term need for financing.

Chapter 17

The U.S. Small Business Administration

No discussion of small business finance would be complete without describing the vast scope of the U.S. Small Business Administration (SBA). Founded in 1953, this U.S. government agency guarantees more than $27 billion in loans to 185,000 small businesses.

What it is. The SBA has a variety of programs in place to support the small business community. It's important to understand that the SBA rarely lends *directly* to a company. When we speak of SBA loans, we mean loans that are made by financial institutions (primarily banks and credit companies) that are *guaranteed* by the SBA. This government agency works with some 7,000 private sector lenders that make these loans available to small businesses. By being an authorized SBA lender, a bank has the option of making a straight loan to a company or placing it under its SBA umbrella. The best known program is its 7(a) Loan Guaranty Program.

A **guarantee** *is a pledge or promise. In financial terms, a* **loan guaranty** *(plural: guaranties) is the instrument used to guarantee that the loan will be paid. Even though spelled differently—guarantee, guaranty—these two words are pronounced the same.*

The SBA also partners with private financial institutions by guaranteeing funds for SBICs (see Chapter 16). It provides loan-guaranty programs to promote export financing (see Chapter 20). The SBA offers procurement assistance by supporting contracts for small businesses and also provides surety guaranties to help small businesses win government construction contracts. It also partners with private-sector lenders through its Certified Development Company program (more in Chapter 19).

In addition to funding assistance, the SBA has business development programs that provide marketing and training information for businesses. It publishes management and technical assistance publications and audio- and videotapes. The SBA also gives information, advice, and help for companies doing export financing, particularly in Mexico, the Pacific Rim, Canada, and Europe. Through its Women Business Ownership program, it makes available mentoring programs, training, counseling, and conferences.

The following are brief descriptions of the key types of SBA guaranteed loans:

7(a) Loan Guaranty Program.   These loans are offered through banks and other financial institutions that are SBA lenders. The loans help businesses to obtain working capital; to construct, expand, or convert facilities; or to purchase buildings, equipment, or materials. The SBA will guarantee 75 percent, or up to $750,000, of a private-sector loan. This means that you can apply for a $1-million loan, and the bank will ask the SBA for its maximum guaranty of 75 percent. The small business completes a loan application to the bank for review. If the bank approves the loan, it is forwarded to the SBA for approval. Upon approval, the loan is funded by the bank, and the borrower has a direct relationship with the lender. The SBA requires that all owners of 20 percent or more of the business personally guarantee the loan.

LowDoc loans.   The low-documentation loan is a one-page application and a quick approval turnaround of up to a few days for loans up to $100,000. To be eligible, the small business can be either a startup or one that has had average sales of less than $5 million for the past 3 years and has less than 100 employees. LowDoc loans have been well received by both lenders and borrowers because of their streamlined documentation procedures. The SBA guarantees up to 80 percent of LowDoc loans.

FA$TRAK.   This pilot program provides SBA guaranties on loans of up to $100,000 and streamlines the SBA paperwork and approval process. The SBA will guarantee up to 50 percent of a FA$TRAK loan.

CAPLines.   This program provides working capital loans for small businesses. The SBA guarantees 75 percent of up to a $1-million loan. There are five different types of working capital lines made available, tailored to the business's actual working capital or seasonal needs. These include:

1. Seasonal line of credit
2. Contract line, which finances the direct labor and materials cost associated with an assignable contract

3. Builder's line, to finance direct labor and materials costs for small contractors

4. Standard asset-based line, generally used by businesses that extend credit to other businesses

5. Small asset-based line, up to $200,000

MicroLoan Program.   This program was developed to provide very small loans from under $100 to $25,000 to small businesses in rural and disadvantaged areas. The SBA makes funds available to nonprofit intermediaries, such as a local economic development organization, which then makes the loans to eligible borrowers.

Minorities and women.   The SBA makes available the Minority Prequalification Loan Program and the Women's Prequalification Loan Program to assist women and minority borrowers in developing viable loan application packages and securing loans. See Chapter 18 for more information.

The fine print: terms and conditions.   The SBA has specific eligibility criteria for these loans. It defines small business by size depending on the type of company and industry. Basically, it wants to make sure that it is making loans to eligible small businesses, not larger businesses that are strapped for cash. Furthermore, the SBA also does not fund businesses that are engaged in speculation or investment. Check with your lender for an updated description of these parameters. The length of these loans is typically five to seven years, and the interest rates are set by the lender (usually around prime plus 2 to 3 percent, subject to an SBA maximum level). And, yes, the SBA *really likes* collateral and frowns upon unsecured lending. It also expects to see you invest cash equity in your business as a precondition of guaranteeing a loan. Finally, as previously mentioned, the SBA requires your personal guaranty if you own more than 20 percent of the business.

How to get an SBA guaranteed loan.   Call your local SBA office and ask for a list of SBA approved lenders in your area. They will send you the list along with other brochures describing SBA services that may interest you. You can then make a loan application directly to one of the lenders they have referred you to. Include the most recent three years of financial statements from your business, and other information as requested by the lender. Once your loan has been approved, the lender will send it to the SBA for approval to receive the SBA guaranty.

To learn more about the SBA, visit its extensive Web site at http://www.sba.gov. You can also phone the SBA Answer Desk at (800) 8-ASK-SBA; the phone is staffed by business information assistants from 9 A.M. to 5 P.M. ET, Monday through Friday.

SBA potential. The SBA has significantly improved its relationships with its banks and has upgraded the programs available to small businesses in recent years. However, there is still a perception that an SBA loan is like a loan of last resort: "I couldn't get the bank to lend me money, so I needed to get an SBA loan." There have been perceptions that an SBA guaranteed loan means giving up your right arm in order to get financing for your business.

Our attitude is, yes, the SBA asks a lot. But if the SBA is your only link to financing, you should be willing to pay the price to grow your business. The good news is that improvements are being made by the SBA. In the world of small business financing the SBA will continue to play an important role. Why? Because when it comes to small business funding, a lot of traditional lenders and investors are still gun-shy—and an SBA guaranty is a government promise to pay.

Chapter 18

Special Interest Financing

In this chapter, we shift our focus from new ways to borrow money to a compilation of money-raising resources for women and minority businesses and other special interest groups. Both the public and private sectors have been interested in providing pools of capital to "disadvantaged" groups. If you fit one of these group classifications, your creativity and willingness to investigate these areas can lead you to a number of interesting sources of capital for your business.

Federal Government Programs

SBA loan programs. The SBA makes available the Minority Prequalification Loan Program and the Women's Prequalification Loan Program to assist women and minority borrowers in developing viable loan application packages and securing loans. The loans are up to $250,000 and must be made to a company that is at least 51 percent women- or minority-owned. These loans are usually made directly through a Small Business Development Center (SBDC) as opposed to a traditional lender. When the loan is approved, it will be referred to a lender who will actually make the loan. At the time of writing, this program is being piloted in a number of cities across the country, and it will hopefully be more readily available in the months ahead.

SBA Office of Women's Business Ownership. This program provides a variety of different training and mentoring programs for women-owned businesses. The Women's Network for Entrepreneurial Training (WNET) is a year-long program that pairs experienced entrepreneurs with less experienced women business owners.

SSBICs. Specialized Small Business Investment Companies (SSBICs) are special interest SBICs. (We talked about them briefly in Chapter 16). They are venture capital firms that are licensed and regulated by the SBA, and provide assistance to small businesses that are owned by socially or economically disadvantaged persons. They operate just like SBICs.

Minority Business Development Agency (MBDA).   This is a federal agency sanctioned under the U.S. Department of Commerce, whose mission is to encourage the growth of minority-owned businesses in the United States. It provides managerial and technical assistance for socially or economically disadvantaged individuals, including Hispanic Americans, Asian and Pacific Island Americans, Alaska Natives and Native Americans, African Americans and Hasidic Jews. MBDA does not provide loans but does work with private-sector companies to increase purchases from minority vendors. If your business qualifies, this may be an opportunity to open up a new client base through the support of MBDA.

Other government sources.   Check with your state and local government to see if there are programs available for women and minorities. You want to find a department that has some combination of the words *women* or *minority* or *business* or *enterprises* or *services.* Have patience: You may be transferred around a few government offices before you get to the right place. When you find the correct office, ask for information about financing for small businesses and they will direct you as to your next steps.

Private Sources

Banks.   There are a number of large and community banks around the country that are targeting women-owned businesses. In some cases they are partnering with other organizations that have a specific interest in women. Some of the country's largest commercial banks are committing annual amounts of money in partnership with such organizations as the National Association of Women Business Owners (NAWBO). Check with your professional associations to see what bank liaisons may exist.

Other lenders.   Asset-based and nonbank lenders sometimes carve out allocations for women- or minority-owned businesses. As an example, Women's Commercial Funding (WCF) is a division of Riviera Finance, a nationwide factor. For more information, call (314) 434-1255.

Women Incorporated.   This is a nonprofit membership organization that partners with the Money Store Investment Corporation, the SBA's largest lender, to steer women business owners to a $150-million pool of capital. This is a resource for women whose businesses are either too small or too risky for other financing alternatives. You can reach them at 2049 Century Park East, Suite 110, Los Angeles, CA 90067; (800) 930-3993; or on the Web at http://data.womeninc.com.

National Foundation of Women Business Owners (NFWBO).   NFWBO is a nonprofit research and leadership development foundation. They compile research that may be useful in your loan proposals, particularly if you want to emphasize your being a woman-owned business. They can be reached at (301) 495-4975 or at their Web site, http://www.nfwbo.org.

Grants.   There are numerous grants that are targeted to special interest groups. Check the resources mentioned in Chapter 21 and look for your particular segment.

Venture Capital.   There are special funds that target women, minorities, environmentally correct, socially conscious companies—you name it. Again, this is a matter of digging through the resource directories (see Chapter 15) until you see ones that may be of interest to you. When you contact them, remember to ask first if these organizations are making new investments at the time. In addition to the venture capital firms mentioned in Chapter 15, you may want to contact:

Women's Equity Fund (WEF).   This Boulder, Colorado–based organization invests between $5,000 and $100,000 per venture. Contact them at (303) 443-7000.

Other resources.   Whatever special interest group you belong to, you'll also want to network within it. Do this locally, as well as at national trade and professional association conferences and conventions. With a little focus and persistence, you'll find a strong underground of knowledge on special interest programs. Often, it's just a matter of connecting to the right people who know people . . . who know people. If you're struggling to find the right association, check with your local library for the *Encyclopedia of Associations.*

Chapter 19

Regional Government Funding

S tate and local governments have what might be thought of as secret pockets of money for small businesses. They don't often advertise that it's available, but on the other hand, they don't intentionally hide it. You just have to look for it.

What are they? Economic development corporations (EDCs) are joint ventures among some combination of state or local government, local banks, private investors, and sometimes the SBA. The main objective is to restore disadvantaged neighborhoods to better status and to bring jobs into the community. One of the attractions to lending money to local businesses under these funds is to increase local employment. Some funds are for special interest groups, such as minority or women's funds (see Chapter 18). In some communities, economic development funds are created simply to support small businesses in the community.

Go to your phone book. The key words to look for are *economic development corporation, business enterprise,* or *community investment corporation.* They will appear under your state government listings and/or your city or township government listings. You might need to look under different categories, such as business development, community development, economic enterprise, or small business. Don't get discouraged if you can't find anything right away. It might also be listed under the name of your city or state followed by *development corporation* (for example, Rhode Island Development Corporation). Also look for information from your state department of commerce.

Chamber of Commerce. If you are having difficulty finding anything, call your local chamber and ask for help. Notices of these types of funds are surely sent to the chamber, as it is the clearinghouse of information for local business owners. The added advantage to networking through the chamber is that you may talk to other business owners who have gone through the process. It's also a strong possibility that you may meet representatives from some of the participating orga-nizations that sponsor the fund, as they have a vested interest in being involved with the community.

As simple as it seems, one of the most effective ways of finding regional government funding is through phone calls, the Internet, and general networking. One phone call or contact will start the ball rolling. Follow every lead, no matter how obscure it seems. Adopting a treasure-hunt approach will make you more open to the possibilities.

How they work.   Economic development funds have some of the eligibility elements of grants. In other words, some funds are very project specific and will lend money to small businesses that are engaged in a specific industry or project. Others are more open-ended in their eligibility. EDCs often work in conjunction with Small Business Development Centers (SBDCs), which can offer assistance in putting together the loan package. There can also be an application fee, depend-ing on the program.

You will need to put together the usual package of business plan, financial statements, and other documentation as part of the approval process. As programs may differ from one to the other, make sure you ask for a checklist of what the EDC will require.

The important point to remember is that these funds are specifically designed for small businesses. These lenders are more likely to loan you money—even if you're a startup—when the more traditional lenders will not. They will take a chance on the fledgling state of your business and advance you cash. Of course, there can be a price for this, so pay attention to all of the details that are proposed as part of the financing.

The more you research, the more you'll find overlaps between what the EDCs are offering and what you might find from SBA lenders. For example, one EDC lender sends a package including information on SBA microloans as part of its information package. Don't worry about which loan belongs to what program; they do intertwine to some extent and your objective is to get the financing for your business.

Sometimes these EDC-type funds will be created to provide avenues to fulfill banks' Community Reinvestment Act (CRA) requirements. Most of those loans are targeted to low- or moderate-income individuals or small businesses. You might check with your bank (assuming it is federally chartered) and meet with the officer responsible for CRA loans.

Contacting EDCs.   Once you have identified some resources, phone them and find out if they are making any loans. Describe your business to them, and ask if it fits their profile. If there is a preliminary fit based on the conversation, they will send you more information. This will usually be in the form of fact sheets and loan applications.

These fact sheets will tell you what constitutes an eligible business, for example:

✓ A minimum operating history of x years and demonstrated ability to repay debt

✓ Whether they will finance startup businesses

✓ Sales revenues that do not exceed $\$x$ million

They will also tell you the terms of the loan, for example:

✓ The amount of the loan (for example, from $5,000 to $100,000)

✓ The purpose of the loan (such as working capital or equipment financing)

✓ Any restrictions (such as a loan/value limit based on certain criteria)

✓ Collateral

✓ Interest rates

✓ Length of the loan

EDCs exist so that small businesses can grow and contribute to the community. Your contact at your local EDC has experience working with people like you, so feel free to ask any question. They will refer you to SBDCs if they think it will help you through the process.

The 504 Certified Development Company Program.   Certified Development Companies (CDCs) are sponsored by the SBA and provide growing businesses with long-term fixed-rate financing for capital assets like land and buildings. CDCs work with lenders to make these loans available to small businesses, and there are about 290 CDCs across the country. Typical projects have different layers of investment: a senior bank loan from a lender, a subordinated loan made by the CDC (100-percent guaranteed by the SBA), and a contribution of at least 10 percent equity from you.

One last thing to keep in mind is that these funds will ebb and flow depending on the fiscal and political climate of your city and state. If you aren't having success finding the right kind of EDC to assist you, wait awhile and try again. The availability is in part dependent on how your mayor or governor views the small business issue. Again, this is why your local chamber can be of tremendous help.

Chapter 20

Going International

For today's entrepreneurs, the world is their marketplace. While you may think that producing goods and services domestically is enough of a challenge, modern technology and business practices enable any company to tap into global resources and markets. Perhaps you want to expand a consulting business into Latin America. Or, you've discovered unique European gift items you want to sell through your catalog company. All of this is within your reach, and there are various financing programs that can help as you take a more global view. In this chapter, we'll focus on exporting and importing, and discuss financing programs that assist entrepreneurs in doing business internationally.

First things first. After identifying the countries that interest you, contact their consulates or chambers of commerce. There you will be able to learn more about doing business in each country, and can get a feel for what procedures you will have to follow. There is generally a lot of paperwork, and these local offices will give you some guidance about where to start.

While we may think of them as two sides of a coin, exporting and importing are two very different activities, and information resources about them come from two different government agencies. The U.S. Department of Commerce can be a valuable source of information about exporting, and the U.S. Customs Services can answer your questions about importing. Contact the Department of Commerce's Trade Information Center (TIC) at (800) 872-8723 or visit them on the Internet at: http://www.ita.doc.gov/tic. Reach the U.S. Customs Services at: http://www.customs.ustreas.gov.

Banks.   If you are going to be either an exporter or importer with a consistent, regular volume, you'll need a bank that can handle these transactions. They are the experts in the documentation, customs issues, and other international details, so make sure you shop for expertise first, not price. If something goes wrong with an overseas order, there is not much you can do 5,000 miles away. The bank, on the other hand, *can* do something. Ask your loan officer about your bank's international capabilities.

A bank expert in international trade can walk you through most of the services you will need to export or import your product. If you're working with a community bank that has limited expertise, ask for an introduction to another bank that can help you.

Importing.   Let's go back to the example of the European gift items. You've discovered some fabulous pottery in a small Greek town and know that your customers will love the uniqueness of the design and materials. You also have learned that the same family has made this pottery in a modest plant in this town for several generations. How do you take this to the next step and import the product? In some cases, you may just whip out your credit card and buy $20,000 worth of dishes, hoping that they arrive off the boat 6 weeks later.

The reality is, however, that you need to be very careful about what you are importing, from where, and all of the associated customs, duties, and tariffs. There are import duties (taxes) on nearly all goods imported into the United States. Don't assume that you can just bring anything in; you need to check first so that your shipment doesn't get held up in U.S. customs. In other cases, the product may be perfectly acceptable in its country of origin, but for use in the United States, it may need to be tested, to have warranties issued—you don't know what might come up. That Greek pottery may have an extremely high lead content, for example, violating government safety regulations or other guidelines.

If you're interested in importing, your best bet is to contact a *customs broker* (found through your Yellow Pages). These individuals are licensed by the U.S. Department of the Treasury and are up to speed on all of the custom regulations, laws, and tariffs. They can help you line up international shipping, ground carriers once the product docks in the United States—all of the details that need to be dealt with when you import.

Often your foreign supplier will require that your bank supply a *letter of credit.* This document tells your supplier that you are prepared to accept the goods and that you can pay for them. The letter of credit essentially endorses you as a bona fide buyer who will pay. The customs broker can also assist you in working with a bank to issue the letter of credit.

Exporting.   When you export a product, your biggest concerns are whether you will be paid by your foreign buyer and whether any political risk will interfere with your business. The U.S. Department of Commerce's Trade Information Center (TIC) should be your first stop. In addition to a fax-on-demand menu of help-ful publications, the center is staffed with international trade specialists who are there to advise small businesses on how to access export assistance programs. The TIC's desk officers will give you a sense of the political risks, and will direct you to the area that can be of immediate assistance. They publish a booklet, *Basic Guide to Exporting,* which is a comprehensive guide of exporting basics and doing business in different countries. To access the fax-on-demand feature or to speak with a specialist, call the TIC's hotline at (800) 872-8723, or visit their Web site at http://www.ita.doc.gov/tic.

State assistance.   You should also check with your *state* department of com-merce. States have an interest in cultivating international trade, and many have developed programs that either lend funds or guarantee trade transactions. Check the government listings in your telephone directory under international trade or economic development.

SBA.   There are a number of incentives to export specific types of products to other countries. The SBA makes available the Export Working Capital Program (EWCP), which is a joint effort of the SBA and the Export-Import Bank. Loans under $833,333 are processed by the SBA, and loans greater than that amount are processed through the Export-Import Bank. The SBA guarantees up to $750,000. There are also U.S. Export Assistance Centers, which offer a full range of federal export programs and services from a number of federal agencies under one roof.

The SBA offers information on how to export, including relevant asso-ciations, country and market information, shipping information, trade leads, government resources, trade law, and much more—all at its Web site at http://www.sbaonline.sba.gov/oit/info/links.html.

Ex-Im Bank.   The Export-Import Bank of the United States, also known as the Ex-Im Bank, is an independent U.S. government agency that helps finance the overseas sales of U.S. goods and services. For example, it provides both guarantees for banks and credit insurance for trade-related loans. It assumes risks that com-mercial banks are reluctant to take for reasons of commercial and political risk. For further information, visit the Ex-Im Bank Web site at http://www.exim.gov, or contact:

The Export-Import Bank of the United States
811 Vermont Avenue NW
Washington, DC 20571
(202) 565-EXIM (3946)
(800) 565-EXIM (3946)

ELAN.   The Export Legal Assistance Network (ELAN) is a program jointly sponsored by the SBA, the U.S. Department of Commerce, and the Federal Bar Association. It provides initial legal services for new exporters for free. The ELAN attorney will help you analyze the export-related legal issues pertaining to your product or service. They also will advise you on options including the SBA and U.S. Department of Commerce's trade assistance programs, export insurance options, international services provided by banks, and other programs that may be of help. For further information on ELAN, visit their Web site at http://www.miep.org/elan. You can find a local ELAN contact through your local SBA District Office.

Running a business with international suppliers or customers is not for everyone, but if your product or service has global appeal, there are many resources to help you sort out your options. Advance communications technology and modern business practices have made global commerce a natural extension for many entrepreneurs—and you may be joining them.

Chapter 21

Tapping Into Grants

Imagine receiving a financial award that doesn't need to be paid back. Sound too good to be true? It's not. Welcome to the world of grants—one of the great untapped pools of money available to entrepreneurs and small businesses. Private foundations, government agencies, and corporate foundations offer literally millions of dollars in grant money tied to specific projects and programs. In this chapter, we explore how you can access this funding source for your business.

How grants work. Generally speaking, grant money is made available for projects and causes that benefit particular interest groups. For example, funds are made available for specific research, development, community development, and other activities. While some people think that finding grant money is akin to looking for a needle in a haystack, your search can be more easily conducted by knowing a few key facts and resources.

Individuals and nonprofit or for-profit organizations can be eligible for grants. The description of the funding will say who is eligible to receive the money. The funding organization is very specific about the use of funds, and it is imperative that you follow the guidelines exactly, or you will be in violation of the agreement. To apply, you'll fill out a grant application, which is typically a long document in which you need to very specifically answer the questions. Some people feel that grant writing is an art, and you may want to tap into your network and find someone who has successfully applied for grants in the past. That person will be able to give you tips on writing the proposal.

Although grants are awards of money that don't need to be paid back, they do come with some strings attached. Grant money must be used for the specific intended purpose, or there is no grant. You'll also be asked to keep detailed records of the project, and document how you spent the grant money. Once the project is completed, the organization giving the grant will want a final report on your achievements.

Related funding sources that give long-term loans are often categorized with grants. While not technically a grant, these loans are usually structured as very low interest rate loans that can be paid back over an extended period of time.

One common misunderstanding is that organizations will give money to you to launch a business. Unfortunately, it's unlikely that you'll find grants for business startup, so you won't want to look into grants until you've been in business awhile.

Where to find grant money.   Organizations that give grants fall into three main categories: private, corporate, and government. Private and corporate funding is generally done through foundations; government funding is through various government agencies. Let's take a look at some of the options available to your business.

Private foundations.   A *foundation* is a nonprofit organization that supports a specific cause or causes. There are thousands of foundations in the United States. A number of them are independent and have name recognition, such as the Ford Foundation or the Carnegie Corporation. Some large corporations have subsidiaries that are structured as foundations. Foundations in general have a charitable or educational focus, and each foundation has a clear mission statement identifying the types of programs it will fund.

Foundations give money to other nonprofit organizations, for-profit companies, and individuals whose approved requests fall within their guidelines and focus. Often the grants are issued for use in the communities where the company does business.

A great resource for information on foundations is the Foundation Center, a nonprofit information clearinghouse, which operates libraries in five major U.S. cities: at its headquarters in New York City, at a field office in Washington, D.C., and at regional offices in Atlanta, Cleveland, and San Francisco. The Foundation Center publishes a number of directories to help grant seekers in their research, including the following:

✓   *The Foundation Directory,* featuring statistical data on more than 7,900 foundations that distribute grants of $200,000 each (or more) annually

✓   *The Foundation Directory Part 2,* featuring data on more than 4,800 foundations whose annual grant programs are between $50,000 and $200,000

✓ *The Foundation Grants Index,* listing over 73,000 grant descriptions for awards of $10,000 or more awarded by more than 1,000 of the largest independent, corporate, and community foundations in the United States

✓ *The Foundation Center's Guide to Proposal Writing,* giving invaluable advice on preparing a funding request

For further information on the Foundation Center, visit their Internet Web site at http://fdncenter.org, or contact them at their headquarters:

The Foundation Center
79 Fifth Avenue
New York, NY 10003-3076
(212) 620-4230

Keep in mind that the timeline for awarding grants can stretch out from several months to a year or more. Each foundation has its own application and review process, and some organizations only review grant proposals at specific times each year.

In addition to patience, creativity is an important ingredient when working with grant funding. Many grant-giving organizations will not fund research or programs that will directly benefit a profit-based venture. That doesn't mean your grant project can't be of benefit to your company, however.

For example, we know of one small business that sold hand creams based on herbs and other natural ingredients. The owner was looking to expand her product line to include creams for children, particularly those that would help heal the burns and cuts that children get so often. Knowing that aloe vera is just one of many natural plants that promote healing in burn victims, she applied for—and received—a grant to research the effects of natural plant ingredients used in healing young children. Her grant project provided her the research she needed to develop her new children's product, as well as giving her valuable connections with scientists and suppliers.

As this story illustrates, you need to think outside the box when you're applying for grant funding as a small business. You're looking for the middle ground that exists between the organization's mission and goals and your needs as a business.

Local government grants.   Many communities have grant money available for special situations. For example, a private individual might have donated money for a specific purpose, such as the rebuilding of retail stores after a fire. Check your state or local government listings under *Department of Business Services* or similar headings to explore local grant availability. Your state department of small business services is another avenue to search for local grant availability.

Laurie Blum has written several books on the topic of "free money." Her *Free Money for Small Businesses and Entrepreneurs* is packed with listings of private foundations, government agencies, and other sources of free and low-cost capital for small businesses and entrepreneurs.

Federal government grants.   Different government agencies offer grants for a wide variety of purposes. Again, this is a situation where you should just dig in and start hunting. As an example, the Small Business Innovative Research Program (SBIR) is a program coordinated by the SBA's Office of Technology. Eligible small businesses are those that are U.S.-owned, employ fewer than 500 people, and whose principal researcher is employed by the business. Businesses receive grants based on innovation, technical merit, and future market potential. Once approved, they go through a three-phase program.

Each year 10 federal departments and agencies are required to allocate a portion of their research and development budget for SBIR awards. These include the following:

- ✓ Department of Agriculture
- ✓ Department of Commerce
- ✓ Department of Defense
- ✓ Department of Education
- ✓ Department of Energy
- ✓ Department of Health and Human Services
- ✓ Department of Transportation
- ✓ Environmental Protection Agency
- ✓ National Aeronautics and Space Administration
- ✓ National Science Foundation

The Small Business Technology Transfer Program (STTR) is a newer program that fosters innovation in the scientific and technological arenas, providing joint venture opportunities between small businesses and the nation's premier nonprofit research institutes. Small business eligibility is similar to that described in the SBIR program, and five federal departments and agencies are required to allocate a portion of their research and development funds for STTR:

✓   Department of Defense
✓   Department of Energy
✓   Department of Health and Human Services
✓   National Aeronautics and Space Administration
✓   National Science Foundation

For more information on the SBIR or the STTR Programs, contact:

U.S. Small Business Administration
Office of Technology
409 Third Street SW
Washington, DC 20416
(202) 205-6450

Or visit their Internet Web site at http://www.sba.gov/sbir.

The key to finding grant money is to research extensively and to put on your creative thinking cap. There's a lot of money available for specific programs. Your business could be one of the lucky ones that is eligible to tap into these extensive sources of capital.

Chapter 22

Private Placements

N ow it's time to *really* stretch your thinking. In this chapter and the next, we discuss funding for established small businesses that need to raise over $1 million. While your business may not yet be eligible for these types of financing, pondering this level of business can open up your mind to future possibilities.

When your company is larger and needs capital to expand, a private placement may be the solution. This is a way to raise money when you are at the in-between stage. At this point, you need an 8- to 12-year maturity on a term loan, which is longer than the banks are going to do. On the other hand, you may not be large enough to tap the public markets for a stock offering or a bond issuance.

What is it? A private placement matches your company (the borrower) with a lender who specializes in longer-term financing (the lender or investor). Unlike traditional bank lenders, the private placement investors do not follow your activities on a day-to-day basis. They will not lend you money unless you have a proven management track record. It is called a *private* placement because your company will not be under the same scrutiny as those tapping the public markets. In effect, by keeping the deal private, you will not fall under the scrutiny of the Securities and Exchange Commission (SEC).

The private placement lender is typically an insurance company or pension fund. These companies invest in debt of growing and middle-market-sized companies. Their funding sources are insurance premiums and pension contributions. They expect a certain return on investment, and, like traditional lenders, the interest rate charged is a reflection of the risk of your company. Private placement financing often means debt, but it can also be equity and mezzanine financing (for more on mezzanine financing, see Chapter 15).

How big do you need to be?   You shouldn't think about doing a senior loan private placement until you need to borrow $5 million. It just isn't cost effective for the lenders to invest their time and resources into a smaller deal. If you present a hybrid deal—one with some layering of senior debt, subordinated debt, and some sort of equity kicker—you can probably go as low as $500,000 to $1 million. You read it here first: You're going to pay big bucks for a deal so small, but it *is* a possibility if you are growing and need the cash.

How does it work?   The first thing you should think about is working with a private placement agent. These are financial intermediaries who originate loans and have relationships with the insurance companies and pension funds. If you're using a larger bank that has a corporate finance department, find out who works with private placements and go from there.

Chances are, some or all of the money that you want for the private placement is being provided by your bank. You need to extend your maturities (lengthen the loan), however, which is not really bank financing. Be prepared that some bankers may feel threatened if you take your term debt to an insurance company. If you are a good customer to the bank (translation: a *profitable* customer), they will be worried about losing the income from your loan. They will not come right out and say this, but know that it may be on their minds.

The agent's role.   Your agent will do a thorough review of your company, industry, market position—everything that you can imagine. Their experience with the investors will give them strong ideas about what will get approved. They will present you with a *term sheet* describing the terms and conditions of what they will propose to the insurance companies and pension funds. You will negotiate that before they even approach the investors—think of it as the first part of the negotiation.

Once you and your agent have agreed to terms, they will prepare an *offering memorandum* to the investors. This is a thorough review of your company; it is a higher-level business plan that answers the key issues a lender might have. Part of the process of putting this offering memorandum together is on-site meetings at your company, including meetings with key members of your management team.

Once you have signed off on the offering memorandum, the agent will send it to a group of potential investors. The agent will be directly in touch with them, answering questions about your company, until there is an indication of interest from enough investors to do the deal. (In a small deal, there will likely be only one investor.) This is called a *soft circle,* meaning that they have approved the deal in concept, subject to their own due diligence.

An investor meeting is arranged at the company, and the management team will present the company to the investors, give tours of the facilities, and answer questions. These discussions give the investors the opportunity to get a feel for you and the rest of your key managers. After this meeting, they go through their formal approval process.

After they have approved the terms of the deal, an *indenture* is created. This is a loan agreement between the company and the investors. Again, the agent is the central point of negotiations. Once the details of the document are resolved, the company signs the promissory note and the deal is closed. Private placements are usually interest-only for the first several years, and then the loan begins to amortize (pay back).

As we mentioned at the top of this chapter, this type of financing will occur only when your company is of the size and growth potential that will interest a private placement lender. As hands-on as an asset-based lender is, the private placement lender is hands-off. They want to put your note in the vault and forget about it. By that very description, your company has to be of the right size and stability to be eligible.

Chapter 23

Public Offerings

Many small business owners think that companies have it made when it's time to go public. *Going public* means that you give up your status as a privately held company and sell stock to the public. You are now accountable to new shareholders, and will be responsible for filing audited financial statements with the Securities and Exchange Commission (SEC). When your company is at this stage, it's a whole new ball game.

Companies go public to raise money for expansion or acquisitions. In making the decision to go public, they are evaluating the financing options open to them as a public company—namely the ability to issue stock to a wide range of investors.

The subject of going public, or initial public offerings (IPOs), is a subject that requires special study on its own. For purposes of this chapter, we will introduce two concepts. Both concepts address public offerings made directly to the public by small businesses, without the use of a traditional underwriter or brokerage firm. One method is a *Small Corporate Offering Registration* (SCOR), where a company can raise up to $1 million. The other is a *Direct Public Offering* (DPO), for companies that need more than $1 million.

SCOR offerings. In a typical SCOR transaction, the business owner manages the whole process from documenting the offering to finding the investors. SCORs are used by companies that are too small for a typical IPO that would have them listed on the NASDAQ small-cap market. In a nutshell, it's a lot of work to get the SCOR offering together and attract investors. Your company may raise up to $1 million in a 12-month period, with some restrictions.

State securities laws govern these transactions, so you need to register in every state where you plan to do an offering. Form U-7 is the general registration form for corporations registering securities under state securities laws. You will fill out the U-7 for each state where you will raise money. A filing of the federal

Form D with the SEC is required on the federal level, with a copy of the Form D required to be sent to those states included on the cover page of the Form U-7.

Form D includes all the basic information about your product, market, plans, and financials. This is the short form of registration, in contrast to the more lengthy offering statements for public offerings. Interestingly, many angel networks (covered in Chapter 14) are using this format for companies seeking capital on the Internet. These forms are on the angel network's Web site and by filling out the standardized document, the registration can be processed for as many states as would be required.

The Form U-7 and the accompanying Issuer's Manual are available free of charge on the North American Securities Administrators Association, Inc. (NASAA) Web site (http://www.nasaa.org), or by mail for $20 to cover printing and distribution costs. Contact:

NASAA
10 G Street NE, Suite 710
Washington, DC 20002
(202) 737-0900 (phone)
(202) 783-3571 (fax)

DPO offerings.   DPOs use the same concept, but only make sense if you are raising $1 to 5 million. Under SEC Regulation A, you can make a DPO offering if your company has up to $10 million in assets. In a DPO, you offer shares of stock to friends, customers—whoever you would like to include. They have been particularly popular when a company has an extensive list of satisfied customers.

The company sends flyers, insert stuffers—whatever is easy and makes sense—along with the shipped product. This is a way to get the word out that the company is doing a stock offering. When people like a product and see this kind of announcement, they tend to want to support the company and will request a copy of the offering statement for review. (Since DPOs are covered by Regulation A of the SEC, you need to file an offering statement.) The customers may then go on to purchase shares of stock in the company.

What you need before doing a public offering.   When you do a SCOR or DPO offering, you are selling to unsophisticated investors. They are not as familiar with the risks of investing in "unknown" companies. It's one thing to invest in Coca-Cola, and another to invest in Julie's Old-Fashioned Cream Soda. Since the investors are investing on somewhat of an emotional level, you need to start with some of the basics: good earnings records, a strong management team, and audited financial statements.

The customers—the investors—want to invest in a product that is easy to understand and, frankly, one that has a little pizzazz. You may have a great idea, but if it is perceived as dull, it won't be well received.

Outcomes.   Unfortunately, there has not been a lot of good news about the outcome of these do-it-yourself public offerings. Many times, the business owner does this as a last-resort type of financing. Raising the money itself can take the better part of a year, and who is running the business while this is going on?

Think long and hard before engaging in this kind of transaction. And do your homework. Talk to someone else who has gone through the process—your best bet is to find a kindred spirit on the Internet. To get started, search on *IPO* or *SCOR financing* on one of the Web search engines.

Chapter 24

Management Strategies— Purchasing

Up to now, we've been talking about where to get money for your business by looking *outside* your business. In this chapter and the following two chapters, it's time to turn an inward glance and review what's happening *inside* your business. We'll review how your management and operations can impact your financial situation—and free up some money for you to put to good use.

When running your business, your hard costs of doing business can be classified into two broad categories: what you make (product), and who makes it (labor). They are all part of your cost of goods as well as the cost of marketing, selling, and managing your business. In this chapter, we'll focus on purchasing strategies that will streamline the cash used in making your product.

If your company manufactures a product, you need to buy materials that go into its creation. Often it costs more to buy these materials in smaller lots, so you want to get very creative about keeping your spending levels in check.

Buy a larger quantity by joining forces with another purchaser. A competitor may be in the same situation as you are. Why not combine your purchasing power and buy your raw materials together? This makes sense if you can significantly reduce your materials cost by jointly buying one larger quantity.

Buy remnants. Take advantage of leftovers. Larger manufacturers buy product in bulk, and if they have anything left at the end of their product run, they either use it the next time, recycle it in some way, or sell it to a broker who will resell it to another market. This happens frequently in the textile industry, for example. Clothing manufacturers purchase fabric for their production and sell the leftover amounts. Small manufacturers buy from these brokers at prices that are a fraction of the original cost.

Buy when you are close to producing.   Don't buy your materials too far in advance, because your money will be tied up in raw materials inventory—and if it's bulky inventory, you'll also incur the cost of storage. Buy your materials as close as possible to when you will be using them to produce the product. The exception to this is if there is a major price advantage to buying in advance. Even so, it makes more sense to have free use of your cash instead of having inventory sitting on the shelf.

A good example of this is a jewelry designer we know who had a major cash-flow problem, made worse by the fact that her business was seasonal. She stocked a large quantity of gems and silver that she held six or nine months before she made the jewelry. She stopped buying gems in advance and tried to buy silver in appropriate quantities when the market price was favorable. These strategies freed up her cash since she no longer had her money tied up in raw materials.

Benefit from your associations.   Many trade associations have cooperative purchasing strategies. They buy products in bulk quantities and pass along the savings by offering their members lower prices than they would normally pay. These products range from lower rates on overnight mail services to discounts at office supply retail stores or on group life insurance policies. Check around when you are joining trade and professional associations and look carefully at what specially priced products and services they offer their members. If you're unsure about which associations may benefit you and your company, check the *Encyclopedia of Associations* in your local library. This incredibly thorough resource has thousands of associations listed alphabetically, by topic, and geographically.

Chamber of Commerce.   Joining your local chamber may provide the benefits previously mentioned, and you will have the added opportunity to network with other business owners. Your chamber may also be a good resource to tap into other local trade and professional groups.

Joint marketing that pays off.   There are many strategies to save money by pooling resources when marketing your product. Let's say you have a service business that you would like to publicize on the Internet. Rather than set up an independent Web site, you can sublet a space on a larger site that is positioned to get more hits from people who are surfing for your service. This will not only cost you less, but you'll be able to benefit from the fact that the larger site is attracting more traffic. Cross-marketing opportunities also represent ways to spend less money. An accounting firm and an insurance agency may team up, for example, and market to the same target customer market.

Decrease your overhead.   There are lots of ways to save money here. Save on long-distance telephone charges by using a telephone reseller. These companies buy long-distance service in bulk, and resell it to businesses. If you have some time leeway, use the U.S. Postal Service Priority Mail instead of the more expensive overnight delivery services. If you serve a global market, U.S. Postal Service Global Priority Mail can offer significant savings over courier services, such as FedEx and Airborne, if you can spare the extra day or two and your packages are relatively small.

If you send many faxes, send them when the phone expense is lowest (usually at night). Use e-mail to reduce phone expense as well—but keep in mind that e-mail doesn't replace voice contact when something is time-sensitive or tone-sensitive. Buy generic office supplies instead of branded ones. You will find that they work just as well! The next time you purchase office supplies, see how much you can save just by going generic.

Recycling opportunities. If you draft a lot of documents, you can save a little money and a few trees by recycling the other side of that paper. Use it again in your printer for drafts or in your fax machine. Another tip is to use the toner saver feature of your laser printer. You print in draft mode until you need a final copy. Your toner cartridge will last much longer by using this feature.

When your business gets larger, you may want to hire a costing consultant to help you save money. They thoroughly examine your expense items and recommend tangible ways to save money. A costing consultant makes sense if your business employs more than 25 people; if it's smaller, the economies of scale generally don't work in your favor. Costing consultants get paid by straight fee or by taking a percentage of the newly generated savings.

Foreclosure Auctions. Need some furniture? Equipment? Fixtures? Look in the classified ads of your local paper for information on foreclosure and bankruptcy auctions. When companies go out of business, everything in their offices and factories is sold to raise cash for their creditors. Because they're looking for a quick sale and cash, you can usually find some good deals. These are cash-and-carry operations, so keep in mind that if you buy some huge piece of equipment, you'll need to be able to take it with you. There are usually truckers lurking in the wings for unprepared customers; if you're caught unaware, it can sometimes cost you more to ship it than to buy it.

Think about how these purchasing strategies apply to your business. They should give you ideas that you can easily apply and implement—and should trigger some additional ones.

Chapter 25

Management Strategies— Employees

Now that you've become creative with purchasing, let's explore how to do the same thing with your employees. In service businesses, the cost of labor is often the biggest expense. Knowing how to minimize your cash outflow while maximizing results is something any business owner can master, no matter what your company's size.

Interns. Whether you are new at hiring staff or need to add people for seasonal projects, think about using interns. They can be high school, college, or graduate students—in any of these cases, they represent a pool of labor that is generally enthusiastic, eager for experience, and anxious to do a good job.

The downside to interns is their lack of experience. Even though you won't be paying them in dollars, one of your responsibilities is to mentor them in their professional development. If you don't have time to have a hands-on relationship, interns may rob you of your own valuable time and cost you more in the end.

"Mommy track." These are professional women who have consciously chosen to downshift their careers in order to spend time with their children. Many of them would love to work part-time, and they can make great employees for small businesses. They usually schedule their time to coordinate with school hours so they can be accessible for their children; for example, a typical work day might be 9:30 A.M. to 2:30 P.M. Think about a mommy track employee for staff jobs that are not time-sensitive.

The little things. There are many little perks you can give your staff in appreciation for the things they do. Small rewards go a long way toward creating loyalty and pride. This could be as simple as recognizing an employee of the month or giving out a modest gift certificate every time someone suggests an idea that results in the business making money or cutting costs.

Looking for creative ways to show your appreciation to employees that go beyond financial rewards? Check out *1001 Ways to Reward Employees,* by Bob Nelson and Ken Blanchard.

Tax-advantaged benefits.   New York City has a product it sells through its transit department called a *transit check,* which is a coupon for subway or bus tokens to be given to employees. The bonus is that the program enables a tax-free payroll benefit; giving it costs your company less than the salary equivalent since it is not subject to payroll taxes. Other cities around the country are also beginning to offer similar tax-advantaged benefits, so check with your local government.

The approach here is not limited to transit costs. The aim is to offer an employee benefit that is a win/win situation: The company doesn't have to pay payroll taxes, and the employee receives a valuable service over and above a paycheck. Your CPA may have additional ideas, gleaned from working with other small businesses.

Stock options.   This is a big feature for employees of many of the burgeoning high-tech companies. You hire people at relatively low base salaries, and give them stock options as a longer-term incentive. People who agree to stock options as part of a compensation package are going to take a long-term view of employment. They know that it takes time for the value of the options to be realized, and that their hard work makes a difference in realizing that value. Whether they are working independently or leading teams, the options affect their work behavior.

When you hire someone with stock options, you need to be very clear that they are giving up some portion of short-term salary for longer-term potential. They need to know that the future is the unknown, and that there are no guarantees that they will become millionaires from the stock options. It is, however, a great strategy for hiring management-level employees when you're strapped for cash. They can jump onto your dream and work to make it happen.

Commissions.   If you need to increase your sales volume to push product out the door, consider hiring salespeople who are 100-percent commission-based. They will get a higher percentage of sales, but you'll only be paying against actual sales made. You'll need to provide product-specific training, and do whatever you can to enhance their sales success.

A variation on this is a low base salary as a draw against commission. The base salary is credited against commissions as sales are made. This gives the salesperson a small amount of financial security through the draw, but still gives him or her incentive to make the sales.

ESOPs.   Do you want to diversify your company's ownership and keep a staff motivated? Try an employee stock option plan (ESOP). This involves selling a percentage of the company to the employees. This gives the company cash in exchange for a strong employee voice in the management and direction of the company. ESOPs can be a strategy to strengthen the company and use the collective resources of the employees to make it work. While this option is typically used by companies with large numbers of employees, the concept can still be used with small businesses.

Outsourcing.   This has been discussed elsewhere, but is worth this reminder: Don't hire full-time staff people until you're sure you can keep them fully occupied. If you don't have a full-time need, either hire part-time workers or outsource the services you need from independent contractors.

All companies have opportunities like the ones we've mentioned here. Whether it is using interns or stock options, these are ways a small business can minimize the cash outlay today. An important caveat in all of this is how you treat the people who work for you. Everyone is looking for acknowledgment and respect, and this is even more important when people are sacrificing in the short term.

Remember to catch your staff doing something right today.

Chapter 26

Management Strategies— Customers and Vendors

There are numerous cash management strategies that involve your customers and vendors. Take the ideas we've gathered in this chapter and see how they apply to your business. Chances are, you'll discover variations on these ideas which will help you spend cash slower and collect cash faster.

Trade credit. Are you paying your suppliers and vendors cash on delivery (either literally or figuratively)? While you may need to do this when you are getting started, set a goal to arrange for credit terms. This means that instead of paying your suppliers right away, you'll be able to pay in 30 days, for example. When you don't have to pay right away, it temporarily frees your cash.

By giving you credit terms, your supplier is actually giving you a 30-day loan in the amount that you owe. This is called *trade credit.* You will probably need to furnish some financial data, including a bank reference.

Trade credit *is an agreement that allows you to pay your suppliers on a 30-day basis, or longer. It can help your cash flow considerably, since you have an extra time period to use your money instead of paying the supplier right away. Trade credit is based on trust and an established business track record.*

Trade credit is one of the easiest ways new businesses can get a break in the early days. Treat it with respect and pay your bills promptly. The good news is that you'll be able to use one supplier as a trade credit reference for another. Over time, you should be able to get trade credit from most of your suppliers, and stretch out the time you can hold on to your cash before paying your bills. A good strategy for growing businesses is to buy small amounts of product from several different suppliers, so that you can establish trade credit with multiple sources.

When you first receive trade credit, pay your bill so that the supplier receives it about five days before the due date. That will show that you are paying a little earlier, and confirms that you are a reasonable trade credit risk.

Customer advances.   What is your customer payment policy? If you don't have one, it's time to establish one (see Chapter 29). If it seems like you're constantly short on cash, one of the culprits may be that your customers are not paying you promptly. You'll always be behind if your customers pay 30 or 60 days after receiving service and you have to pay your suppliers and employees right away. Here are some approaches you may want to try:

- ✓ *Payable on delivery.*   You make a sale, you collect right away. No payment, no sale. You can accept payment either in cash, credit cards (if you take them), or checks.
- ✓ *Down payment.*   You agree to a project with a client and ask for a certain amount up front to get started. This could be 25, 33, or 50 percent of the total price.
- ✓ *Hybrid.*   You collect half on delivery and the rest in 15 or 30 days.

Credit cards.   Many small business owners resist taking credit cards because they perceive the fees as being too expensive. If you're in a business where your customers keep asking you if you take credit cards—and you don't—you may be giving away business just because of your perception of the costs of credit cards. This is an example of being penny-wise and pound-foolish. Ask your banker to refer you to someone in the bank who handles *merchant card services* (that's what the ability to accept credit card payment is called). You'll need to fill out an application with the usual financial information. In addition, you'll describe the product or service that is being sold, including an estimate of what you think your monthly credit card sales volume and average transaction size will be. If mail-order sales will be only a portion of your credit sales (you also sell at trade shows, for example), be sure you communicate this, in relevant percentages, to your bank.

You'll have a higher probability of success with your bank if you have a relationship (in other words, if you have been doing business there for over a year). If your bank denies you merchant card status, there are independent service organizations (ISOs) that you can call. While it may be the only way to get up and running, keep in mind that ISOs are likely to collect slightly higher setup fees and transaction fees than your local bank. Do your homework here, because some ISOs are in business to take advantage of entrepreneurs who seem desperate. When shopping around for service packages, be sure to compare prices for buying (or leasing) the terminal, the printer, and other necessary hardware. Prices can vary wildly from one company to another. Keep in mind that the necessary hardware can be purchased separately—you don't always have to get it from your ISO.

As of this writing, there is still discrimination against granting merchant card status to home-based businesses. This is because home-based businesses need merchant status primarily for mail-order sales, and the mail-order industry has a record of credit card complaints. When your banker knows you won't be able to verify a customer's identification face-to-face, they can be reluctant to extend merchant status. The more professional you are in the way you present your company, and the more stability your business has, the more likely this will not be an issue.

Sponsorships. Suppose you're working on a huge project where you need some funding. Think about which corporations could benefit from the audience you are targeting, and consider putting together a proposal for corporate sponsorship to finance your work. Underwriting your project is a way the corporation can get visibility—even a public relations benefit—from working with you.

As an example, you may be putting together an industry conference. Corporate underwriters can sponsor different parts of the event. For instance, a local printing company could be the underwriter for the continental breakfast. At the breakfast, they would have an information table where they could pitch their services. In addition, you could acknowledge on the conference brochure that the printing company sponsored the breakfast.

There are an infinite number of variations to this idea. The keys to success are to figure out who could benefit from your project and then approach them to explore the idea. It must be a win/win—you want the sponsor to feel that their participation is valuable, not just because they are investing, but because they will be a valued partner in the project. Your proposal needs to clearly point out specifically why it's in their best interest to support your efforts.

Barter. Business-to-business bartering is a cashless option for many entrepreneurs. Businesses today conduct more than $13 billion in bartered sales each year, for items ranging from airline tickets to office supplies and design services. You can either barter one-on-one with another company or join a barter exchange. Upon joining an exchange, you will "deposit" an amount of your goods or services and commit to a certain amount of trade during the year.

Let's suppose you have a business providing accounting and bookkeeping services. By joining an exchange, you would contribute a certain number of hours of accounting services, valued at your hourly rate. In turn, you would be able to withdraw an equivalent amount of services that are among the offerings of that exchange. Keep in mind that bartering is not about getting discounts; rather it is a way to receive services that you need, paid for by services you render.

Bartering can be the perfect way to conserve cash while growing a business. Keep in mind that barter transactions fall into the *in-kind* services area of your taxable income. Any barter transaction should be included on your tax return.

Barter exchanges are listed in the Yellow Pages under *barter.* Some of the largest organizations include Trade Exchange of America, (248) 544-1350; Barter Advantage, (212) 534-7500, http://www.nate.org/baine1/htm; Barter Corp., (630) 268-2820; and the Illinois Trade Association, (847) 390-6000.

You may want to subscribe to *Barter News,* a quarterly publication that has been the Bible of the industry since 1979. Contact them at (714) 831-0607, or at their Web site, http://www.barternews.com.

The trade association overseeing the barter industry is the International Reciprocal Trade Association (IRTA). Founded in 1979, they provide a range of services to members wanting to establish a barter exchange. Contact them at (312) 461-0236, or on the Web at http://www.irta.net.

The National Association of Trade Exchanges (NATE) offers training, information, and general support for businesses operating or starting exchanges in their area. For more information, contact them at (216) 732-7171, or visit their Web site at http://www.nate.org.

Chapter 27

Financing Strategies to Buy a Business

In the chapters up until now, much of our focus has been on financing strategies to start and grow a business. Sometimes, however, you'll be better off buying a business rather than going through a startup. There can even be more financing alternatives available to you this way.

Going concern. A business that's up and running, and has employees, customers, assets, and liabilities, is called a *going concern.* The term refers to the fact that a business can continue to operate, or keep going, during a purchase or sale. In contrast, a company in the startup phase is not a going concern. If you tried to sell a business before it's established, it wouldn't have value to a potential buyer.

When you're starting a business, the issue of seed money is usually a challenge. Instead of spending all your efforts on launching a company, maybe you can switch gears and see what's already operating that's similar to what you want to build. Look around. Network. Read the classifieds in your local paper. Find a business broker who matches buyers and sellers. Talk to your friends and associates about what you're seeking.

Finding a business. Let's say you've found a business that you'd like to pursue. Work through the broker and learn as much as you can prior to meeting the principals. You want to get all of the financial data as well as information on the market, the customers, and the employees.

When you meet the owner, be prepared with questions, but be more prepared to *listen.* Pay attention to the words, the body language, and the tone of voice he or she uses. Notice where there is a sense of pride, and observe where comments are sketchy or veiled.

Keep in mind that there is always an "official" reason to sell a company, but there also might be a hidden agenda. For example, you may have found a seemingly ideal retail business on the main street of a nearby town. All of the elements are strong, and the situation seems too good to be true. It may be! Dig deep and learn if zoning laws have changed, or if a major chain store is going to take over in the next block. Do your homework.

Once you've decided that it makes sense to buy the company, you have several options. You can go to your bank and see how they can help in acquisition financing, and you can also speak to the owner directly about seller financing. This is where you would give the owner a down payment, and he or she would finance the sale under some negotiated terms.

There are advantages to seller financing. First, it's probably less restrictive than a bank loan. Second, it gives you the opportunity to continue contact with the owner on a regular basis. Third, if you run into a problem with the business and have trouble making a payment, the owner may be more understanding.

For all of the personal reasons why it makes sense to work with the seller, there are also downfalls. If he or she is really tired of the business, there may be a level of impatience in dealing with you. Similarly, the seller may be intolerant of any challenges you face in the future.

Bank financing will involve a thorough evaluation of the company, as you would expect. In addition to working with your own bank, you may also want to talk to the seller's bank, especially if there has been a long and good relationship. That bank already knows the business and just needs to become comfortable with you. If you use bank financing, be prepared for a term-loan agreement with appropriate covenants. Chances are high that this will be a secured loan, and you may have to add your personal guarantee to close the deal. (See Chapter 28 to review these details.)

It may seem like you're taking on a lot of debt, but remember that you're buying a company where you can make money from day one. You have none of the issues of starting a business from scratch. You're paying for the time, experience, goodwill, and mistakes that the seller has already put into the company.

Buying a franchise.   Another possibility is to buy a franchise. Franchised businesses are those that recreate a company's concept, products, and operations on a regional or national scale. When you buy a franchise, you're buying a brand and a proven business operating method that has worked successfully for others.

Many entrepreneurial magazines devote sections or entire issues to the franchise world. Start reading these sections, and look for their annual top 100 or top 500 franchise businesses. Get a sense of what is being offered and how it could fit into your business strategy. Think about a business that has demonstrated success but is not yet on every corner in your town.

The advantage of a franchise is that someone else has already figured out the formula of what works. Think about this: You can go into a McDonald's anywhere in the country—in the world for that matter—and you'll see the same setup, the same basic menu, and the same process, often run by *teenagers*. That's the power of franchise operations.

When you buy a franchise, you purchase the franchise for your area, and you also pay a franchise fee, or royalty, to the franchisor on a regular basis. This is usually calculated as a percentage of sales of your franchise. This franchise fee is your payment to have the use of that system and process in place.

The due diligence process (a thorough investigation of the company) for buying a franchise is like that for buying any business, and you want to get an attorney who specializes in franchises to represent you. A legal document called the Uniform Franchise Offering Circular (UFOC) is a required document that all franchisors need to issue upon offering franchises for sale. The UFOC guidelines were prepared and adopted by the North American Securities Administrators Association (NASAA). Go to NASAA's Web site at http://www.nasaa.org to become more familiar with the UFOC.

If you're in the early stages of reviewing franchising opportunities, you may want to check out *Tips and Traps When Buying a Franchise*, by Mary E. Tomzack. This guide helps novice buyers make decisions about which franchise to buy, how to finance it, and what questions to ask. Tomzack, a franchise expert, also shows how to navigate through the legal maze and around first-year stumbling blocks.

When you buy a franchise, sometimes the franchisor assists with the financing, and other times you'll be on your own. Look into bank financing as well as SBICs for funding. Specifically ask if the lender does franchise financing. If it doesn't, ask for referrals to lenders who can help you. Of course, check with your chamber of commerce for referrals as well. Make sure your attorney is familiar with the purchase of franchises, as this law is somewhat specialized.

There are hundreds of Internet sources on franchise financing, many of which are specific to individual states. Here are three sites to start your research:

American Franchisee Association (AFA)
http://www.vaxxine.com/franchise/afa

National Financial Services Network
http://www.nfsn.com

Women in Franchising (WIF)
http://www.vaxxine.com/franchise/wif

MONEY—
PREPARING
TO GET IT

Chapter 28

Are You Bankable?

In creating this book, we knew that readers would want to know *where* to get money for their businesses right away. So we put those chapters up front in Section 2, and up to now we've explored with you numerous traditional and unconventional money sources.

But just as important is *preparing* to get the money—defining the strategies and putting together the financials and documentation that make you and your company a good candidate for funding. In this chapter and the seven that follow, we show you the tools to prepare yourself and your business for your new "partners"—the individuals and institutions investing in your business.

To start, keep in mind that banks and other investors almost always look to your personal credit as an integral part of the approval process for business loans. In fact, the system called *credit scoring* (discussed in Chapter 10) is increasingly being used by banks as the key component in the decision to lend for loans of less than $100,000. Your personal credit history is integral to the credit scoring system, thereby making it a key variable in the credit decision process.

Credit reporting agencies. Take the time to see what the major credit agencies are saying about you. You are entitled by law to receive a copy of your credit report, and we recommend that you request copies from at least two of the major services. It will take about two weeks for your credit report to arrive. When it does, spend some time reviewing it and report any errors immediately.

The different agencies may report different information, and comparing a few of them is a good check and balance for yourself. If there are any mistakes, you can then take action to correct any incorrect information prior to initiating contact with a bank or other lender.

The credit report will tell you how much credit availability you have. This is important because lenders evaluate your creditworthiness based on the total amount of credit *available*. For example, if you have several department store charge cards, a couple of MasterCard and Visa cards, and some gasoline cards, the bank will assume that you've fully utilized these lines of credit, even if your balance is currently zero. When doing this review, don't be surprised to find credit for stores or bank cards that you stopped using years ago. Take time to clean up the credit lines and make room for your business.

If you've been denied credit within the past 60 days, you can order a complimentary copy of your credit report from the agency whose report resulted in the denial. If you haven't been denied credit and just want to check your report, you can do so for a modest fee (usually around $8). All of the following toll-free numbers are menu driven, and you can conveniently order a copy of your credit report with a credit card.

Here are the numbers to contact the top three credit reporting agencies:

Experian (formerly TRW), (800) 682-7654
Equifax, (800) 685-1111
Trans Union, (800) 916-8800

The credit report will also indicate how promptly you pay your debts. If you are consistently on time, this will be reflected. If you are often 30 to 60 days (or more) past due, the lender is going to be wary of lending money based on your payment history.

Your credit versus your company's.   You may be saying, "Why does my *personal* credit history matter if *my company* is the borrower?" It matters a lot! Small businesses are viewed as being virtually interchangeable with their owners, even if you've chosen to operate as a corporation. While the borrower of record may not be you personally, the lender is still psychologically thinking of you and the company as one and the same entity. The more steps you take to create a management team and a strong outside board of directors, the more you will be viewed as running a business instead of the business being you.

Credit cleanup.   Here are some tips for making sure that your personal credit is in shape. It's best if you can implement these ideas early in the process.

✓   Get copies of your credit report from two of the major agencies (see sidebar on this page). Review each item carefully and contact the agencies with your questions. If something needs to be adjusted, such as removing a credit card that is no longer being used, ask for their guidelines to request the changes. Then make sure you see a follow-up report after the change has been instituted. Make it a habit to check your credit report annually.

✓ There may be a temptation to respond to credit card offers that come in the mail. Be careful with this. Remember, the bank will add up your total credit *availability,* so you don't want to use up future credit needs by impulsively responding to credit card solicitations.

✓ If you have a lot of personal credit outstanding, make sure you pay at least the minimum requirement each month, on time. High personal credit balances will not necessarily penalize you, but not paying the minimum requirement on time will show up on your credit report and deter lenders from considering your request.

✓ If you have a *limited* credit history—for instance, if you've never had a credit card in your own name—consider a strategy to establish credit. You may want to purchase something on an installment basis, for example, and repay the loan on a timely basis.

✓ If you have a tarnished credit history, you may want to work with a personal credit specialist to take steps to clean up your credit. Business owners who are in this situation would be wise to use the services of a professional, because in this case, the damage from the past could negatively influence your company's bankability. Call the National Foundation for Consumer Credit at (800) 388-2227 and ask for the name of a Consumer Credit Counseling Service (CCCS) in your area. These organizations provide counseling and helpful information on how to budget and manage your finances.

Guaranties. Often, you will be asked to personally guarantee one of your company's financial obligations. This can range from a loan to a commercial lease. By signing a guaranty, you are promising to make good on the obligation *no matter what happens* to your company. Be careful before signing guaranties—make sure your attorney reviews the language. Know that the obligation under the guaranty will show up on your credit report. As an example, if you sign a 5-year lease for a design studio, your total obligation under that lease (the monthly rent times 60 months) is your personal liability. If you go out of business, you are still personally responsible for paying the remaining rent under the lease.

The personal guaranty is a fact of life in small business. You may not have to issue them all of the time, but in the first three to five years, there is a greater likelihood that you will need to guarantee. As your company grows and you have a demonstrated track record, you'll have stronger negotiating power to eliminate the guaranties the next time the corporate obligation is renegotiated. To help you negotiate better, here are some tips:

✓   Make sure that you and your banker agree—in writing—about the ranking of your guaranty. In the event of a default, you want to make sure that the bank first acts to liquidate collateral rather than acting on your guaranty. This means, for example, that they would take possession of the equipment that you put up for collateral before asking you to pay out of your own pocket.

✓   Try to negotiate a cap on the guaranty (for example, up to a certain amount of money).

✓   Negotiate the exclusion of certain assets (for example, your personal residence) in the guaranty.

✓   Negotiate in advance for a release of the guaranty once certain financial benchmarks have been met.

Credit enhancement.   What happens if your credit is not satisfactory in the eyes of the creditor? You can utilize someone else's credit. You can ask a spouse, a parent, or a friend to guarantee or cosign a note. If you need to do this, just remember that this person's creditworthiness will have to meet the criteria of the lender.

One small business owner we know used her husband's guarantee for her company's line of credit during the first several years of operation. The "Bank of Bob," as she called this arrangement, gave her the ability to establish her company's creditworthiness with the imprimatur of a strong guarantor behind the scenes. Once her business had established a track record on its own, the bank shifted the guaranty to her company instead. When this happened, it was a happy day for her (and her spouse!), and a sure sign that her business was growing stronger.

As the stories of many entrepreneurs show, personal credit habits directly translate to your business. Lenders will be much more comfortable with you if you cultivate your company's credit as if it were your own. We don't want you to shy away from taking calculated risks—instead, we want you to be positioned in a bankable way so that you'll be able to raise what you need, when you need it.

Chapter 29

Customers, Collections, and Concentration

There's nothing like the feeling you get after making a big sale. Unfortunately, many business owners don't apply the same enthusiasm and persistence when it comes to collections and getting paid. We think this is poor judgment, because making the sale becomes meaningless if you don't collect what is owed you. In this chapter we'll take a look at invoicing, collections, and other elements that greatly impact the financial picture of your business. We'll also give you strategies and tools that will help you keep your collections and cash flow running smoothly.

When small businesses are getting started, they often don't think about invoicing and collections policies—they're so happy to make the sale, they just accept the money whenever it comes in. The savvy business owner, however, establishes clear guidelines from the beginning. How strong is your invoicing and collections process? Answering the questions that follow can help you shape an effective receivables policy.

Invoicing and terms of sale. What are your terms? COD? Half upon order, half upon delivery? Credit for 30 days? Make sure that your terms are clearly stated on the invoice, including any policies pertaining to returns and exchanges, use of retainer hours, and other details. If there is any interest on past due accounts, this should be clearly identified as well. It is important to be *consistent* in your terms; when you start making exceptions, your controls begin to crumble.

Customer credit. As a business owner, it is your responsibility to know enough about your customers to determine their creditworthiness. You may research your customers yourself or use a credit agency, such as Dun & Bradstreet, to determine the payment history. Keep in mind, however, that the information from a credit agency may be outdated and may not reflect current financial weaknesses in the company. The important thing is to make sure that you know enough about your customer to give you comfort that you will be paid.

Dun & Bradstreet has created a Small Business Services group to address the needs of small business owners. They've tailored their traditional big business services to meet small business' needs for low-cost credit information, collections, and marketing. You can order a report of your choice at any time for a reasonable fee without any subscription agreement, and no minimums apply.

Businesses can also list themselves with D&B at no charge—fees are paid by the companies obtaining information on your creditworthiness. For more information, contact D&B's Small Business Services group at (800) 552-3867 extension 1067, or visit them on the Web at http://www.dnb.com.

If you want to do a credit check yourself, you will need to know your customer's bank. Call the bank and ask for either the credit department or the account officer who handles the account. Use a friendly and unassuming tone in asking your questions. These can include the following:

✓ How long has the bank had a relationship with this customer?

✓ What is the average balance in the checking account?

✓ Does the bank extend credit to this company?

✓ When did the bank last review this company?

✓ Has the customer complied with the terms and conditions of any loans?

If doing this makes you uncomfortable, by all means have an outside credit agency do this for you. It is worth paying a small fee instead of seeming anxious when talking to the bank. Tell the credit agency, however, that you want current information.

The "It's a big company, I'll get paid" myth.   Your customers may be large, publicly held enterprises, but that doesn't mean that you'll get paid right away. There are countless stories of small businesses that have sold products or services to large companies—anxious to have these big names as clients—only to read in tomorrow's newspaper that their big client just filed for bankruptcy protection. Some industries are notoriously slow payers. For example, small businesses in the fashion and design world have learned that selling to department stores may mean two, three, or more months before being paid. Do your homework and assume nothing.

Sales to individuals. If your company is essentially a retail business selling to individuals, you have three main ways of being paid: cash, checks, or credit cards. You need to decide what you will accept and establish controls to protect yourself. For example, it may be worth investing in merchant card services so you can accept credit cards, since you get immediate cash payment from the credit card merchant. The cash flow gained may be more important to you than the few percentage points that you pay in fees.

Operational follow-up. Once the sale is recorded, make sure you have good systems in place to track the next steps. If you are extending credit (that is, the customer will pay at some future time after receiving goods or services), establish a system to send reminder notices of future payments due. Keep a list of customers who are perpetually past due or who consistently bounce checks. This will be a *watch list* that will help you monitor and anticipate any long-term payment problems.

We have all either claimed or been told that "The check is in the mail." When a customer says this, make sure you follow up after allowing an appropriate amount of mail time. If the excuses continue, know that they are usually buying time. If the customer is physically located in your town, and the amount warrants your or another manager's time, tell the customer that you'd be happy to facilitate the collection by stopping by their office at a designated time to pick up the check. One owner of a design agency flew 1,000 miles to a client's office, camped out in the lobby and worked on his laptop until the client finally paid the large, past due fee.

Check policy. If you accept checks, establish a clear policy for collecting information from your customers. You may want to use a service that checks the customer's bank balance prior to your acceptance of the check. Keep in mind, however, that a positive bank balance at the time of a phone call doesn't mean that money will be in the account when the check is processed for collection. In that case, you'll need guidelines pertaining to bounced checks. Often you'll call the customer and ask if the bank should resubmit for collection. If you want to collect a bounced check fee, this should again be clearly stated on the invoice so there are no surprises. Bounced checks tend to cluster around the same customers. You may decide that after two bounced checks, transactions will need to be paid for in cash, on delivery. Again, the specifics of your company's policy aren't as important as having guidelines in place for systems that work for you.

Past due accounts. In spite of the best-laid policies and plans, sometimes there are past due accounts. If you've established a system, your controls will give you reminders to send follow-up past due notices. If a customer ignores your invoices, you'll need to initiate follow-up phone calls. Some of these customers will avoid your calls. The key here is to be firm, but not threatening. If a company hasn't paid, it's either because they are grossly dissatisfied with the product or service they purchased, or they are having cash-flow problems.

The dissatisfaction situation can be avoided by a simple customer service procedure: In the week following the completion of the sale, call the customer to make sure he or she is happy with what was purchased from you. If there *are* any negative issues, they can usually be fixed right away. The secondary benefit to this strategy is that your client will be favorably impressed that you actually took the time to follow up.

If you know your customer is satisfied and you still haven't been paid, then you're most likely dealing with a cash-flow problem. Assure your customer that you want to work together to bring this to a win/win resolution. You may need to construct a payment plan, for example. If you're getting paid smaller amounts—but on a regular basis—that is certainly better than getting zero percent of the full amount. If all else fails, you may need to engage the assistance of a collection agency. These firms are typically compensated based on a percentage of the amount collected. While these percentages are often high, your choice may be 40 percent of something rather than 0 percent of the invoiced amount.

Call the Commercial Law League at (312) 781-2000 for referrals to a local, reputable collection agency. There are many people who say they are in the collections business; you want to make sure you're dealing with someone professional and ethical.

Concentration of customers.   When you launch your business and make your first sale, that means 100 percent of your sales have been made to one customer. Now, while we agree that it's good business to build repeat business, we also feel strongly that it's also critical to diversify your client base. A rule of thumb is that no one customer should represent more than 10 percent of your total sales in the course of the year. When a customer represents a disproportionate amount of sales, then you run the risk of really being hit hard if that business goes away. There's safety in numbers.

You may be thinking that you have the best relationship imaginable with this client. That may be the case, but the client may merge with another company, your main contact may get downsized, a project could be placed on indefinite hold—anything could happen to upset the harmony of that relationship.

Banks and other lenders are also going to be looking at the concentration of customers. They pay attention to that 10-percent threshold and will actually discount the value of larger customers to give them a worst-case scenario view of your business. If a bank is looking at the worst-case scenario, shouldn't you be thinking about it also?

Collection and concentration policies are the financial backbone of any business strategy. Clear policies and procedures can put you on solid footing now and help you avert future difficulties.

Chapter 30

Business Plans

There are dozens of "how to" books and resources that cover the subject of business plans, and we encourage you to investigate several so you can discover which ones are a good match for your specific business and your personality. Instead of detailing the process of writing a plan, this chapter will focus on an often-overlooked element—the *strategies* to use when creating business plans.

Purpose. First, be clear on why you're investing the time and/or money to write one. Business plans are used primarily for one of two reasons: to raise money, and to provide an operating blueprint for running the business. When you're raising capital, all lenders and investors will expect to review a complete business plan. Do not expect them, however, to always thoroughly study your plan; in many cases they want to see that you have taken the time to think through the key aspects of your business from a strategic perspective.

Because the business plan is such an important element in obtaining financing, we recommend that you seek help in putting it together. This will cost you anywhere from nothing to over $20,000 depending on who assists you. There are a variety of resources available to you, as detailed in Chapter 35.

The Process

The easiest way to write a business plan is to assemble all of the component information ahead of time. Be very clear on the answers to these questions:

What is your vision of the business? Your vision is the big picture of how you see the business several years in the future and how your product or service will actually impact the market it serves. You should be able to envision this image in full sensory detail—so much that you can see it, hear it, taste it, smell it, and feel it as if it were real today. Not everyone will ask you about your vision, but having a clear, passionate answer will give a distinct message that you have a long-term view of being in business.

What is your company's mission?   This is more than listing the products and services your company provides. It is the heart and soul of why you are spending all of your time and talent in your business. Your mission statement should really answer the question of what business you are *really* engaged in. For example, a day spa provides a variety of services to its clients, but its mission (the *real* business) may be to provide a respite for busy executives to replenish in a peaceful, supportive environment.

Who is your ideal target client/customer?   A lot of business owners fool themselves into believing that they can be all things to all people. That is short-sighted. Create a profile of your ideal client or customer, including the appropriate psychographic data (for example, where they shop, what restaurants they eat in, where they vacation, what their hobbies are, what they spend disposable income on, and so forth). When you are clear about who your target client is, then the client will be much easier to identify. Moreover, you immediately become more referable as people get a better understanding of who your typical customers are.

Who is your competition?   Lenders want to know with whom you compete, and you will be better at what you do if you understand your competition. Find out who your five biggest competitors are. Learn what makes them good, and see where and how you do things differently. Knowing your competition also provides you with resources to whom you can outsource work if you do not have the staff available for a big project. Lenders will view this positively.

What are your financial projections?   Your CPA or business consultant can assist you in creating realistic projections of your company's balance sheet, income statement, and cash-flow statement. There are two key things to know about projections. First, the past does not equal the future. Just because your company has had a particularly good or bad year does not foretell a rerun in the next year. Second, the projections are only as good as the underlying assumptions. Create a page of assumptions and attach these to the plan so that the lender or investor knows your frame of reference.

The Contents

Business planning texts will go into the details of how to organize the information. They usually include sections that look like the following outline:

✓   Executive summary

✓   Table of contents

✓   Description of the business (include a description of your product or service, the concept, and your unique selling proposition)

✓   Market analysis (customer profile, industry information, analysis of the competition, market size, etc.)

✓   Marketing plan (sales strategy, pricing, advertising, and promotion)

✓   Company operations plan (nitty-gritty description of how the business operates)

✓   Management team/board of directors (bios and relevant experience)

✓   Professional support (attorney, CPA, banker, business consultant, insurance broker, etc.)

✓   Risk factors and their mitigators

✓   Financial plan (historical financials, projections, and assumptions)

A note about the executive summary.   The most important section of the business plan is the executive summary—and that section is written last. The executive summary tells the reader *what* the company does, *who* you are, *where* the company is expected to go in the coming years, *why* you want the money, *how* the funds will be utilized, and *when* the money will be paid back. Make sure that your executive summary is a compelling statement—after all, how can you expect anyone to read further if they are bored from the beginning? You want this section to shine. The rest of the plan, then, provides all of the details to back up what is stated in the summary.

The act of creating a solid business plan is well worth it. You will identify strengths in your strategy that you may not have previously seen. And, you may zero in on some weaknesses that you had completely overlooked. If you've gathered all of the essential information ahead of time, the actual writing of the plan will flow easier. Creating a business plan that you use as a blueprint for running your company may be one of your best investments of time and money. Make sure that your writing is clear and understandable. Give in-depth information about your product and service, but don't make it too technical. Business plans that are steeped in jargon will be put aside. The reader (a potential investor, perhaps!) is not going to sit side-by-side with a technical glossary to translate key information into understandable English.

A living document.   You'll find that there are aspects of your business plan that are obsolete by the time you complete the process. That's fine—your business is supposed to grow and change. Think of the business plan as a living document that is fine-tuned as your business develops. Think about revising it every 6 to 12 months, depending on what kind of changes are occurring. The revisions will flow a lot easier than the original document, and the plan will continue to provide a road map for the future.

If the process of writing a business plan overwhelms you, you'll find some resources to assist you in Chapter 35. If you use outside help, though, remember that it's *your* vision and business, and *you* must be the driving force behind the plan's creation. As you work with someone, make sure that is always in the top of their mind.

Chapter 31

What the Bank Is Looking For

The explosion of small business startups and expansion has created a "money hunt" for entrepreneurs. In response to this increased demand for funding, many financial institutions have created systems for efficiently reviewing small business loan applications. While each lending situation is unique, many investors utilize some variation of evaluating *the five Cs of credit* when making credit decisions: character, capacity, capital, condition, and collateral. In this chapter, we'll take a look at each of these ingredients and how they may impact your funding request—and ultimately the success of your business. Review each category and see how you stack up.

Character. What is the character of the management of the company? What is their reputation in the industry and the community? Investors want to put their money with those who have impeccable credentials and references. The way you treat your employees and customers, the way you take responsibility, your timeliness in fulfilling your obligations—these are all part of the character question.

This is really about *you* and *your* personal leadership. How you lead yourself and conduct both your business and personal life gives the lender a clue about how you are likely to handle leadership as a CEO. A banker will be looking at the downside of making a loan. Your character immediately comes into play if there is a business crisis, for example.

As small business owners, we place our personal stamp on everything that affects our businesses. Often, banks do not even differentiate between us and our businesses. This is one of the reasons why the credit scoring process evolved, with a large component being our *personal* credit history.

Capacity. What is the borrowing history and track record of repayment? How much debt can your company handle? Will you be able to honor the obligation and repay the debt? There are numerous financial benchmarks, such as debt and liquidity ratios, that investors evaluate before advancing funds. Become familiar with the expected pattern in your industry. Some industries can take a higher debt load; others may operate with less liquidity.

Robert Morris Associates (RMA), the leading organization for lending and credit risk professionals, is an excellent resource for comparative business data, including financial benchmarks and ratios. Each October, they produce a financial reference book, *Annual Statement Studies,* which features financial data on more than 400 industries. Using this guide, you can evaluate the ratios that are typical for businesses in your industry and see how your company compares. Priced at $125, the publication often can be found in local business libraries. RMA can be reached at (800) 677-7621, or on the Internet at http://www.rmahq.org.

Capital. How well capitalized is your company? How much money have *you* invested in the business? Investors often want to see that you have a financial commitment and that you have put yourself at risk in the company. Both your company's financial statements and your personal credit are keys to the capital question. If the company is operating with a negative net worth, for example, will you be prepared to add more of your own money? How far will your personal resources support both you and the business as it is growing?

If the company has not yet made profits, this may be offset by an excellent customer list and payment history. All of these issues intertwine, and you want to ensure that the bank perceives the business as solid.

Conditions. What are the current economic conditions and how does your company fit in? If your business is sensitive to economic downturns, for example, the bank wants a comfort level that you're managing productivity and expenses. What are the trends for your industry, and how does your company fit within the trend? Are there any economic or political hot potatoes that could negatively impact the growth of your business?

Collateral. While cash flow will nearly always be the primary source of repayment of a loan, bankers look at what they call the *secondary source of repayment.* Collateral represents assets that the company pledges as an alternate repayment source for the loan. Most collateral is in the form of hard assets, such as real estate, office equipment, or manufacturing equipment. Alternatively, your accounts receivable and inventory can be pledged as collateral (this is described in more detail in Chapter 11).

The collateral issue is a bigger challenge for service businesses, as they have fewer hard assets to pledge. Until your business is proven, you're nearly always going to pledge collateral. If it doesn't come from your business, the bank will look to your personal assets. This clearly has its risks—you don't want to be in a situation where you can lose your house because a business loan has turned sour. If you want to be borrowing from banks or other lenders, you need to think long and hard about how you'll handle this collateral question.

It's worth repeating that while each of these elements is a key component, investors in small businesses pay particular attention to *you,* the owner/operator. Even if you're incorporated, they will always look to your personal credit, and they'll want a clear idea of how you handle your personal financial obligations. They'll also want to know what happens if something happens to you.

This is a critical concern if you're a solo entrepreneur. Being solo doesn't means that you won't be able to get money—it just means that you need to prepare a plan that will convince investors that you have all bases covered in the event that you cannot perform your responsibilities. Pointing to a strong board of advisors and some powerful strategic alliances will go a long way to offset the perceived weakness of being the only real decision maker.

Another way to look at this is to simply think through the scenario of what *would* happen to the business if you became ill or disabled for a period of time. What would you do? How would decisions be made? How would the business function without you? Go through this exercise and create a crisis management plan. This will benefit your business strategically and will be excellent preparation for facing the issue with a lender.

Keep in mind that in evaluating the five Cs of credit, investors don't give equal weight to each area. Lenders are cautious, and one weak area could offset all the other strengths you show. For example, if your industry is sensitive to economic swings, your company may have difficulty getting a loan during an economic downturn—even if all other factors are strong. And if they don't think you're a person of character and integrity, there's little likelihood that they'll make the loan, no matter how good your financial statements may be.

As you can see, lenders evaluate your company as a total package, which is often more than the sum of the parts. The biggest element, however, will always be *you.*

Chapter 32

The Language of Money

W hen you're just learning financial terminology, it can appear to be as easy to understand as ancient Greek! Take heart, though—like any language, it can be learned. As a business owner, you'll make more progress with investors if you are conversant in some basic financial expressions. Here are some tips to break the barrier from regular conversation to financialspeak.

Getting Started

Getting your feet wet. When you're learning something new, it's always easier if you do a little bit at a time on a frequent basis. An easy place to start is by getting familiar with the financial news. Start reading the business section of your local paper. By reading articles about local companies, you'll ease into the lingo while also becoming familiar with your local business community. As you read on a daily basis, try to learn one new word or concept, then try to apply it to your business. If this sounds like a lesson in how to build vocabulary, it is. Another source of information is the business news on radio or television. It is the same concept, just a different medium.

Going national. After you feel more confident, take it to the next stage and read national periodicals. The *Wall Street Journal* and *Investors Business Daily* are two daily newspapers that focus entirely on financial news. *Business Week, Fortune,* and *Forbes* are national financially oriented magazines. You will be pleasantly surprised to see how much you will begin to understand just by doing this regularly.

Take a course.   Adult education classes offer a variety of programs on small business topics. Take the plunge and sign up for one on financial strategies. An introductory accounting course will get into the nitty-gritty of accounting language, and you'll also develop a framework for how your books should be set up. When you take a class, it's a good opportunity to talk to others in the new language. This is no time to be shy—virtually everyone there is taking the class to improve their knowledge and understanding.

Annual reports.   Another learning tool is to read annual reports of companies in your industry. You will learn more about what the big guys are doing, and you'll also learn what financial lingo is most often used. The business section of your library has copies of annual reports, and of course, you can also do this on the Internet. Go to the Hoover's Web site (http://www.hoovers.com), for example. It has reports on thousands of publicly held companies.

Moving to the Next Level

In the next phase, you can move into areas that are specifically germane to your business and industry. In addition, you will start to follow economic benchmarks that directly impact your business.

The credit markets.   There is a lot of attention given to interest rates in the financial press. The short-term bellwether is the *discount rate.* This is the rate that the Federal Reserve charges its member banks to borrow. When the discount rate goes up, it eventually affects the *prime rate,* which is the rate that banks charge their corporate customers.

You will also hear about the *bond market.* The *long bond,* which is shorthand for the 30-year U.S. Treasury bond, gets a lot of press, as it is the bellwether of the direction long-term interest rates are going. This has an impact on everything from fixed mortgage rates to the ups and downs of the stock market. Corporate bonds and other treasury bonds are followed in this market.

The *yield curve* gets a lot of attention. It's a charting of yields on treasury securities, ranging from 3-month bills to the 30-year bond. Typically, the yield curve is upward sloping, meaning that yields get higher with longer maturities. When the shape of this changes—for example, it can flatten—it impacts investors' decisions on investing short-term rather than long-term.

By being more familiar with interest-rate movements, you'll have a better understanding of why lenders charge what they do, and even when to anticipate increases. If your banker perceives that you have an underlying familiarity with rate fluctuations, he or she will view you as a more sophisticated customer—it just adds to your knowledge and your perceived professionalism.

The stock market. Why pay attention to the stock market? Because it will indirectly have an impact on when and how lenders and other investors view your company. If there is a *bull market* (when stock prices are consistently going up), angel investors may be less inclined to take risks in unknown companies because they can get great returns from the stock market. In a *bear* market (when stock prices tend to be depressed), investors look for alternative investments to stocks, and they often flock to bonds. This is referred to as a *flight to quality.* In those times, investors perceive that it is safer for them to be more heavily invested in bonds than in uncertain stocks.

---

*Confused about how to keep bull and bear markets clear in your head? Think of a **bull market** as charging ahead, which represents an actively advancing stock market. A **bear market** is one in hibernation, with little movement or a decline in stock prices.*

Economic indices. Every week announcements are made about numerous indices that impact interest rates and their underlying markets. Economists, bankers, and other financiers pay careful attention to everything from unemployment statistics and the consumer price index (a measure of inflation), to new housing starts and the producers price index (a measure of manufacturing productivity).

The more you familiarize yourself with these indices, the more you'll see which have the most impact on your business. You may think that your business is too small to be affected by these. That's not true. You need to put your business in a global context in order to grow it. The smallest thing you learn could be extremely helpful in your overall strategic planning.

Commodities. Knowledge of commodities pricing and fluctuations has direct bearing on your company if you either buy commodities to make your product or sell to companies whose pricing is affected by commodities. From precious metals to agricultural commodities to oil prices—start following the relevant ones for your business.

Foreign exchange. If you are selling in dollars and getting paid in another currency, you need to pay attention to the foreign exchange markets and currency trading patterns. A country's currency is affected by many economic factors, and knowledge of foreign exchange is just one of the necessary pieces of your business puzzle.

Now, don't panic. No one is saying you need to be an expert in these areas. Understanding the language of money is all about building small pieces of knowledge, one step at a time. Even the most advanced financial pros are always learning something new. By making a commitment to expanding your financial vocabulary and knowledge, you'll be a much more savvy business professional.

Chapter 33

Presenting to Investors

In previous chapters, we've discussed what an investor will be looking for when you apply for funding. In this chapter, we offer the specifics on *what* to present and *how.*

When it's time to actually present to lenders or other investors, you want to emphasize the content of your package. You also want to present yourself and other members of your management team as first-class professionals. These presentation issues are partly substance and partly style, but together they form the foundation for a successful outcome with people—strangers, essentially—who are considering investing money in your business.

Printed Presentation

Your package. The investors will tell you what they want to see. Provide them what they request, and if you're missing information, tell them ahead of time. They'll probably want to see your information in its entirety, not delivered to them on a piecemeal basis. In their enthusiasm, some business owners overdo it, and give the investors reams of unwanted information. Avoid this paperwork deluge; stay with the rule of giving them what they have asked for. Here are some common elements to include:

- ✓ *Business plan.* They will usually ask for this. You shouldn't even be thinking about raising money without having a well-developed business plan.

- ✓ *Financial statements.* Investors will ask for around three years of financial statements. Make sure they are neatly and clearly photocopied, so they can be easily read.

✓ *Personal financial information.*   You may be asked for this, although they might just run a credit check on you. As a business owner, it's a good idea to update your personal financial statement every year.

✓ *Company brochures.*   Prepare a set of your marketing materials so your banker can see how you are presenting your company.

✓ *Press package.*   If you've received some publicity about your company, prepare a small press kit with some of the key articles.

Now let's take a look at some general guidelines for all of these components. First, think *substance,* not fluff. What is the image you are conveying in print? Look at the components in your presentation package, and objectively review each one for content. Second, make sure someone has read through everything for typos, incongruities, grammatical errors, and so forth. Third, all components should be neatly prepared and displayed. If you don't have the in-house capability to prepare a professional-looking package, hire a secretarial support firm or other service to do it properly. Think of how you would feel if someone gave you a package that was poorly copied and had coffee stains on it!

Objectivity.   We all have a tendency to lose perspective when we're in the throes of a big project. Ask a trusted colleague, friend, or advisor to review your investor package. Solicit their feedback and respond to it appropriately. Remember, you don't have to do this alone.

Oral Presentation

Dress for success.   The business world has become much more casual, but the world of banking and finance has not. While there are certainly regional differences in dress, plan to wear appropriate business attire to your first meeting. If the investor dresses casually, you can do so on the next visit. First impressions are important, so make sure you present yourself as a business professional.

Be prepared.   You may think you have written everything imaginable about your business in the plan, but the investors are going to want to *hear* what you have to say about your business. When you answer their questions, they will be looking at *how* you talk about the business. They want to experience your passion, your drive, your ambition. This isn't a time to be shy—it's the time for you to enthusiastically tell what needs telling.

Brush up on your most recent monthly or quarterly financial figures and know how they compare to the same period last year. Give clear answers to questions about your competition. They will be evaluating how well you really know your competition by how you respond. Prepare explanations for all of the key risk factors of the business. You don't need to solve each one, but know that the investors will be focusing on the risks. If you cannot adequately address them, it might end any further discussions.

Positioning.   Small businesses, by definition, are companies that do not dominate their markets. But the way you *position* your business will tell the investors a lot about how you view your business world. Take time to position your company within the context of your bigger vision. Investors are more comfortable with people who have a strategic view, rather than a short-term perspective. They'll be looking for ways, too, in which you demonstrate the uniqueness of your product or concept.

On-site visit.   Invite the investors to visit your company. This can be important, even if you are home based. Give them the opportunity to experience how you do what you do. Having an on-site visit is a way you can enhance your professionalism by showing them how your business operates.

Psychology of selling.   In a nutshell, you need to sell them so they can sell you to their colleagues. We're not talking about a hard sell. Rather, you need to clearly, succinctly, and passionately tell your story in a way that it can be retold to a loan committee or other investors. This is about taking a mass of numbers, statistics, and market strategy and synthesizing it in a way that can be clearly understood and repeated to others. Have all of the data to back up your story, but be able to create compelling soundbites that represent the essence of the business.

Networking.   When you meet other professionals at association meetings, you never know when you will meet someone who represents a connection to an investor. All of these presentation tips apply in a networking environment. Have a succinct 15- to 30-second soundbite prepared describing what your company does and what you're looking for. These are not formal presentations, but your delivery can make the difference between just a casual conversation and the introduction to a great contact.

Think of yourself as "on" any time you're in a business or professional situation. This is not to say you'll be phony. But as long-time entrepreneurs who have a keen understanding of how funding happens, we both know that a new acquaintance sitting next to you at a business function may end up being a future investor in your company—or may give you a direct connection to one. If you make networking behavior automatic, you might surprise yourself with the results!

Chapter 34

The Patchwork Approach to Financing

N ow that you know more about financing and cash conservation strategies, it's time to look at them in a real-life context. This chapter will show you how theory translates into reality, and the role of creative persistence when it comes to finding the money your business desperately needs.

Where to begin.   When you decide that you need money, one of your first exercises will be to decide *how much* you need and to justify that amount. Start with the immediate need for cash. For what purpose do you need money and what is the appropriate amount? Is the money to offset working capital shortages? Do you need to buy equipment? Is the business expanding? Once you've figured out the amount, take time to work through a budget and see if the amount you're targeting is going to be enough.

One of the challenges small business owners face is *underestimating* the amount of a borrowing need. It makes it much more challenging to return to a bank after you have been there a month earlier, and say, "Oops, I made a mistake in the amount." It's much better to take a thorough look from the beginning.

Perhaps you need a high-speed copier in your business. After shopping around, the one that interests you is $20,000. You have done some research and decide to lease rather than buy the copier. The lease payment comes out to $400 per month. That is clearly an easy number to slide into your budget. But is there anything else to think about? Is the insurance included, or is it extra? How many cartridges will you go through per month? If the copier needs to be repaired, will they provide a loaner, or will you have to go without a copier for a week?

The key to this exercise is to imagine all related costs that surround this new copier. After factoring in all of the accessory things, that monthly payment looks more like $500 than $400. And $100 can be a big deal to a small business owner, so that differential is *not* insignificant.

This thinking can be applied to any investment decision you make, no matter how small your company. The message is to take into account *everything*—add it up—and see how comfortably the business can handle this new expense item every month. Using the copier example, this business owner found it to be a highly worthwhile investment for the business, given the amount of high-speed copying that was being outsourced to the local print shop. He knew that the expense of sending out the work coupled with the labor cost of his assistant running back and forth and checking everything was becoming expensive to his business. Bringing the copier in-house made a positive difference.

Patchwork approach.   One of the most creative things a small business owner can do is to take a *patchwork* approach to raising money and managing cash. As you review all the choices from Section 2, think about how you can create the best financing package for your company without being wedded to only one or two techniques.

This is an exercise in thinking outside the box—by exploring the myriad alternatives, you may come up with a totally different end result than what you expected when you began the process. The following story is a striking example of one business owner's experience.

John owns a business that produces molded metal components used in the manufacture of a variety of industrial products. He had a long-term relationship with his bank, and his credit facilities included a line of credit and a term loan. His banker, however, had recently left and he was working with a new account officer.

The business had been growing steadily, but then a major crisis occurred. Due to uncontrollable circumstances, two of the company's largest clients left within a couple of months. One customer moved its manufacturing facilities overseas, and the other stopped making the packaging that required the components supplied by John's company.

This resulted in a 35-percent drop in revenue that could not be replaced quickly. John recognized the trouble and engaged in several activities simultaneously. First, he did a detailed line-by-line review of the company's expenses. He cut costs and stretched cash to improve the manufacturing productivity in the plant. Next, he went to his bank and asked for a restructuring and increase in the term loan. The bank denied his request. Even worse, the bank insisted that to maintain the relationship, he would need to put additional equity (his own cash) into the company.

John was not in a position to contribute equity, because he was already deferring his own salary as a way to reduce expenses. Through networking within his community, he found an economic development corporation that was willing to structure a subordinated loan with warrants (discussed in Chapter 15). The interest rate on the debt was 12 percent, but once he factored in the impact of the warrants, the implied interest rate was a whopping 40 percent. While the company absolutely needed the money, he could not in good conscience commit to this extremely expensive option.

His next stop was the regional office of the SBA. The SBA officer directed him to several banks that were SBA lenders in his area. Ironically, his bank was the region's largest SBA lender, but it was still insistent about the additional equity. After more negotiating, he was able to close an SBA term loan with another bank—without committing to additional equity.

John's time was completely focused on this refinancing for six months, during which time the business limped along. It was not until he completed the refinancing that he was able to go back to the business of marketing, so that he could rebuild revenue. Today the volume is nearly back to where it was before the drop.

Lessons learned.   John learned some important lessons from this rocky experience, and every business owner can benefit from his hard-won wisdom. Here are some outcomes from the situation:

- ✓   John learned the value of having a diversified customer base. While it had been great to have two large customers contributing so much volume, here was a classic example of what happens if you lose one or more of those customers. As the business rebuilds, John is getting more customers whose individual accounts do not constitute more than 10 percent of his revenue.

- ✓   As the business was not prepared for such a crisis, John found that his time as CEO was completely preoccupied by the refinancing, and as a result the company's marketing efforts suffered. He is now deepening his management team so that all of the burden no longer falls solely on him.

- ✓   John learned that relationship banking works when there is a *depth* to the relationship. He had a strong connection with one person at his original bank, but that person left. Now he is building trust and rapport with several officers at his new bank as a safeguard in these times of mobile careers.

- ✓   John is now preparing for the next step, which is to find some equity investors. He is making connections through his personal network and is also exploring angel networks. Given his recent experience, he knows it is not too soon to start this process.

As John's story demonstrates, it's important to be open-minded *and* persistent in evaluating financing options. Even though at this point you can't imagine getting your business into such a dire situation, none of us knows where our entrepreneurial road may lead us. Armed with the knowledge of financial options—different types of loans, stringent cash management, or even a new bank—you'll be able to save your company from possible disaster. But you need to be prepared for downturns. What can you do to better prepare your company?

FOUR

MONEY—HOW TO MANAGE IT

Chapter 35

Resources for Help

B y now you may be overwhelmed, and thinking, "How am I ever going to figure all this out?" Yes, it can be a little daunting to face so many new ideas and challenges. Take heart—you're not alone. Most small business owners seek some type of help in the early and growing stages of their businesses. Fortunately, there are many resources available to help you. Here are a few to get you started.

Small Business Development Centers (SBDCs). SBDCs are counseling centers that are partially funded by the SBA. There are approximately 1,000 centers around the country, and many of them are affiliated with local colleges and universities. They provide management assistance to startup and growing businesses and will help you in preparing loan applications. They have a special expertise in the documentation pertaining to SBA and other government agency loans. SBDCs are jointly supported by the private sector, the educational community, and the federal, state, and local governments.

SCORE. The Service Corps of Retired Executives is a program partner of the SBA. It utilizes the services of retired and active executives to assist small business owners with free and low-cost management and business counseling. One of the services they provide is assistance in developing a business plan. Business counseling services are now available by e-mail, and many of the centers provide seminars on the subject as well. For quick, reliable information, including the Find SCORE tool that lets you locate the nearest SCORE office for business counseling face-to-face, visit SCORE on the Web at http://www.score.org. Or call (800) 634-0245 for the location of the SCORE chapter in your community.

SBA. You've already learned about the scope of lending services available from the SBA (see Chapter 17). In addition to guaranteeing loans, the SBA is a massive clearinghouse of information that is invaluable to entrepreneurs. The agency offers a full range of support programs on the national, statewide, and local level. Its Web site, http://www.sba.gov, is a user-friendly, jam-packed central resource, and it should be one of the first stops for small business owners on the Internet. The SBA also sponsors a toll-free information service, the SBA Answer Desk, at (800) 8-ASK-SBA. A call to this number can get you free information brochures, the location of the SBA office nearest you, details on SBA services, assistance in tracking down the right SBA program, and much more. Contact the SBA regional center in your community to learn about classes and seminars they host on a variety of small business topics.

Internet.   One of the beauties of the Internet is its equalizing nature. Companies can be multinational conglomerates or one-person home-based enterprises and have Web sites that are accessible to anyone in the world. The Internet has spawned hundreds of sites that serve the small business community. If you are looking to make connections on the Internet, use the major search engines and find sites that come up under *small business.* Many entrepreneurs have established sites that are dedicated to serving the small business community.

A growing number of corporations and national periodicals also have established Web sites or subsites dedicated to addressing the financial needs and interests of small business owners. Among the most valuable are the following:

American Express Small Business Exchange
http://www.americanexpress.com/smallbusiness

Center for Entrepreneurial Leadership at the Kauffman Foundation
http://www.emkf.org

Dun & Bradstreet
http://www.dnb.com

Entrepreneur magazine
http://www.entrepreneur.com

Fast Company magazine
http://www.fastcompany.com

Idea Factory (sponsored by Ernst & Young)
http://www.ey.com/idea/default.htm

Inc. Online (the online companion to *Inc.* magazine)
http://www.inc.com

Intuit (makers of the popular financial software Quicken and QuickBooks)
http://www.quicken.com/small_business

Mastercard International
http://www.mastercard.com/smallbiz

Money Online (the online guide to *Money* magazine)
http://www.money.com

The Edward Lowe Foundation
http://www.lowe.org

The Entrepreneur's Wave
http://www.en-wave.com

Entreworld (from the Kauffman Foundation)
http://www.entreworld.org

VISA International
http://www.visa.com/smallbiz

The *Wall Street Journal Interactive Edition*
http://www.wsj.com

Working Solo Online
http://www.workingsolo.com

The Xerox Small Office Home Page
http://www.xerox.com/soho.html

Trade and professional organizations.   Some of the best places for information and advice are networks of your peers. On a local level, your Chamber of Commerce exists to serve businesses in the community. If your chamber is not small-business-friendly, you can still make connections that will lead you to area organizations that support small businesses. Associations for your particular industry are a good way to keep up with news and opportunities. If you haven't connected with one yet, check out the *Encyclopedia of Associations* at your library, or the professional trade journals in your field.

Another option is to join one of the many small business associations, and attend their regional or national conferences. These gatherings offer an opportunity to meet business owners from many different industries, and the exchange of ideas can be very fruitful. Most associations have Web sites; some time spent with one of the major Internet search engines will lead you to full details of a group's mission and member benefits. You can also find valuable links to other sites from an organization's site. Who knows—that valuable contact you need may be only a mouse click or phone call away!

If you're looking to expand your business resources and connections, be sure to check out the companion volume in the Working Solo series, the *Working Solo Sourcebook*. It's filled with details on more than 1,200 valuable business resources, including books, audios, publications, Web sites, associations, government agencies, services, supplies, and much more.

Adult Education Centers.   Community colleges and centers for adult education (such as the Learning Annex) are increasingly conducting classes on business topics, such as bookkeeping and how to write business plans. Check schedules for class availability, and select one where you know you will be able to fulfill the time commitment. This option is a group setting rather than one-on-one, but it represents an economical way to boost your business knowledge. An added bonus is that you'll be able to meet other entrepreneurial types who can share their ideas, experiences, and advice.

MBA programs.   If your community has a university with a graduate school of business, explore ways you can tap into this resource. Inquire whether they offer classes to individuals not enrolled in a full-time program. They also may be a good source for interns to work in your company. A number of schools work with local businesses looking for assistance with business plans and marketing program development. The interchange offers students a real-life look at how a business operates, while providing valuable information for you. Some of the schools will provide the work pro bono; others will charge fees for the service. Four-year business colleges can be another option. To begin the process, call the dean's office to find out how the school may be working with small businesses in your area.

Alumni organizations.   Your alma mater may have a local organization in your community. Reconnect with your college or graduate school colleagues and see if the local club has an entrepreneurs committee. This is an excellent resource for both support and networking opportunities. And if your alumni group does not have a small business or entrepreneurs committee, why not take the initiative to start one? It could help all of you address small business issues as your businesses grow.

Private business and management consultants.   There are thousands of individuals who consult on financial, marketing, strategic planning, human resources, and technology aspects of new and growing businesses. Consultants tend to charge on an hourly basis; if you expect to use one on an ongoing basis, consider asking for a retainer arrangement. That way you won't be charged every time you pick up the phone to ask a question.

Why use private consultants? Because they're professionals, and that's what they do for a living. While the volunteers who staff a number of the small business agencies are bright and earnest in their desire to help small business owners, they are not necessarily experts. Consultants can be pricey, but if they can help you short-cut some of the learning curve that lies ahead in your business, they're well worth the investment.

Many of these professionals prepare business plans and will create a customized plan based on your objectives. In some cases, they'll work with you as you meet with potential lenders; in other cases, they'll help prepare you for the meetings. Expect to pay from $5,000 to over $20,000 for this service. Interview several consultants before hiring anyone, and make sure that you are completely satisfied with the service once you begin working together.

Software. There are many software packages that walk you through everything from creating a marketing plan to managing your finances. Pick ones that are user-friendly and have direct applicability for what you need. For example, you might select a program that gives step-by-step assistance with writing a business plan. The software gives you a great start in clarifying your thinking, and then you can seek specific assistance for help in creating a loan proposal.

Tapping into these resources will help you sort through the maze of money matters that small business owners face. As a secondary benefit, you'll receive guidance and support on other general management issues that your business will face as it grows—and you'll undoubtedly meet some interesting entrepreneurial minds along the way.

Chapter 36

Bookkeeping and Beyond

Organizing your financial records is the foundation for creating systems to track cash and make financial projections. It doesn't matter how sophisticated your books are; what's important is keeping *consistent* records. Once you have your books organized, you can then advance to the next step and put systems in place to monitor and control the financial flows.

Organizing Your Books

Commit to upgrading one level. Do your "books" consist of a bunch of dog-eared receipts stuffed in a disintegrating shoe box? If this sounds like your business, don't despair—that's how you have chosen to organize until now. The key is for you to commit to upgrading your organizational system at least one level. We'll describe some different levels, and you can decide which one will be the appropriate one to aim for in your business.

Basic tracking. Any stationery or office supply store sells bookkeeping supplies. Dome Publishing puts out two products that will take you beyond the shoe box in a very respectable fashion for as long as you do manual accounting. One is called the *Approved Expense Account Diary.* This weekly expense account diary can be used by salespeople and executives. The beginning of the diary has a summary of the current IRS guidelines for expenses, including the necessary documentation.

The second Dome product is the *Simplified Weekly Bookkeeping Record.* It contains a weekly record of income and expenses, including whether expenses are deductible. It also features a weekly payroll record and a summary page that can be given to your accountant. It is very user-friendly, and is an appropriate introductory system for a business owner who is less familiar with the book-keeping process.

Filing the receipts.   Now that you're tracking on a more organized basis, the next thing to consider is what you *do* with all of the documentation and receipts that you need to save. You can make files for each general category, and simply insert the appropriate receipts into the folder. As your business grows, you may need to have folders for each month. Your receipt categories should follow the same categories you use on your tax returns. That way it will be easier to access all of the necessary information when you're preparing your returns.

Overwhelmed by all the clutter in your office and frustrated at the tax deductions you're losing because your receipts aren't organized? Check out *Taming the Paper Tiger* by professional organizing consultant Barbara Hemphill and the Paper Tiger software at http://www.thepapertiger.com. You may also want to contact the National Association of Professional Organizers (NAPO) at (512) 206-0151 to locate a professional who can come in and set up efficient paper systems for your office.

Computerize.   The next level in bookkeeping control is to purchase an off-the-shelf software package that is suitable for your business. There are many popular versions that have different features, ranging from checkbook-type personal finance programs to fully integrated accounting packages.

If you're confused about which to buy at the early stages, ask your accountant if he or she has a preference. The leading computer magazines also run frequent reviews of new programs and comparison rating guides. One of the benefits of computerization is the ability to hand a disk to your tax preparer at the end of the year. So, if your accountant has a preferred software choice, it can often make sense to use the same program.

More sophisticated software.   You may use a simpler accounting program in the early stages of your business, and move up to a more advanced software package as the business grows. You'll know if you have outgrown your software if you find yourself making many manual adjustments and inserts. Again, talk to your accountant about what to purchase. You may also invest an hour with a financial consultant whose expertise is matching software packages to particular businesses. Ask around through your network for someone with this expertise. As accounting software packages are proliferating, it represents an opportunity for accountants to specialize in a way that differentiates them.

Custom software.   You're probably a long way from this option. But if your business is experiencing hypergrowth or has some unique accounting quirk, it may be worthwhile to invest in a custom accounting program that will capture your company's characteristics.

Business Services

Checking account.   In the early stages of your business, most accounting will be based on or around your checking account. It's where you'll be depositing receipts for goods and services sold, as well as disbursing most of your payments. It's important that you have a business account separate from any personal checking accounts. There are several reasons for this. First, it establishes a baseline of professionalism and the recognition that you take your business seriously. Second, it keeps business and personal financial issues separated, as they should be. Third—and perhaps the most compelling—if your business ever is audited, you'll want to make sure that *only* the business is audited. If everything is commingled, it will open the door to scrutinizing your personal records as well.

Other bank services.   These range from online banking services to automatic monthly payroll tax deductions. If you have a large seasonal cash buildup, you may want to use a money market or investment account when that balance is high. Cash management services, such as lock boxes, may be appropriate if you have a retail business that receives frequent check payments by mail. Banks also provide trade finance services, such as letters of credit, if your company imports or exports goods.

If you maintain a substantial balance in your checking account (say, $10,000 or more) and you want to avoid the process of frequently moving money in and out of investments, inquire to see if your bank has cash management checking accounts available for small businesses. These accounts automatically sweep extra funds into interest-bearing investments each evening, enabling your money to work for you even when you sleep! You'll pay a higher annual fee to have such an account, but if your balance remains large enough, the interest you'll earn will more than offset these fees. The accounts also frequently include other banking services, such as a free safe-deposit box.

Bookkeeper.   A bookkeeper can do a variety of things to support you. It's an easy service to outsource, so don't worry if you don't have enough volume to justify hiring a full-time bookkeeper. This person should have some basic training in the subject and should have some experience—as a growing business, you don't have time to train a newly minted bookkeeper. These professionals can keep the books, reconcile your bank statements, and write your checks (for your signature, of course). Your bookkeeper should also be able to handle basic payroll responsibilities. To find one, ask your CPA for referrals, and network with other business owners in your community.

Payroll services. This is an outsourced service whose sole function is to handle payroll services. They disburse the money, pay the required federal, state, and local taxes, and file the appropriate quarterly and annual payroll tax returns. If you have more than a few employees, this specialized service is well worth it because it removes a big headache that business owners face on a regular basis. There are a number of payroll services available; Paychex is one, however, that specializes in small businesses. You can contact them at (800) 322-7292 or through their Web site at http://www.paychex.com.

Tax preparation. Tax preparation and determining estimated taxes is one of the primary services an accountant can provide in the earlier years of your business. (You'll find more about working with an accountant in Chapter 43.) With tax laws under constant change, consider a financial professional who's up to date on tax law changes a "must" for your business.

These are the basics to get your records in order and to provide the foundation for budgeting and financial projections. While bookkeeping and other record keeping may seem like tedious tasks, taking an active, positive stance in this area will definitely pay off now and as your business grows.

Chapter 37

Establishing Controls

D o you know where your money is? That is, if you took inventory today, would everything add up? Or would you find funds, inventory, supplies, or other items missing? If this thought makes you cringe, you're not alone. Losses due to mismanagement and theft can happen in any business. The answer is not to deny the possibility, but to set up systems that prevent the losses from occurring in the first place.

The area of controls is one of the important areas of cash management. If you don't have controls in place, money will literally fall through the cracks. Whether you're operating solo and forget to deposit checks, or are delegating to a growing staff, you need controls to provide the necessary checks and balances for your business. Too many small businesses have learned the hard lesson of employee embezzlement or theft. Creating controls from the beginning will minimize any potential losses.

Invoicing system. One of the more common mistakes that new businesses make is misplacing their receivables. You complete a job, and then can't recall if you ever billed the client. Avoiding this situation (a cash-flow nightmare!) doesn't require any complex system. Just create an invoice for every sale, and keep it in a specific file called *receivables* until you get paid. If you don't invoice for services, you'll find that two, three, or even six months have gone by and you haven't been paid. Whose fault is that if you don't have a collection system in place?

Even worse, a check comes in from a client, and it gets buried in a pile on your desk. Two months later, you vaguely recall that you never got paid for services and think that the customer stiffed you. Again, you need a system to track what's been invoiced, what's been paid, and what remains due. This is so simple, yet in the early stages of many businesses no thought is given to creating a system to collect what has been earned.

These failings are not limited to novice business owners. If your company's collections currently aren't under control, examine the systems you have in place and see how they might be improved. Remember, if you're not collecting promptly, you've essentially moved into the banking business—giving free loans to those who owe you money. Set up a system and collect what's due you.

"It will never happen to me."   How many business owners have said this, only to find out that their best and brightest employees are stealing right underneath their noses? This usually happens when the owner is preoccupied by a thousand different things as the business grows. The scenario usually involves giving more financial responsibility to a trusted employee. Once the owner feels comfortable with the transfer of responsibility, the fatal mistake is made: The owner totally trusts the employee and doesn't use any form of checks and balances.

Here are some ways this can happen. Let's say you have a retail business where a lot of cash changes hands. The person handling the cash register will not record one small sale a day. Similarly, maybe your business has inventory that has a street value, and small amounts of inventory disappear gradually. On the surface, these incidents may not seem like a great loss. But even the tiniest bit of skimming over a long period of time can add up—and can result in serious damage to your business.

Here's a potential scenario if you're in a service business where you're traveling all of the time. Checks come in from clients and are deposited by your trusted employee. Every once in a while, though, a check doesn't make it to the checking account because it was cashed by your employee.

When there's a lot of activity happening, you might not know this is going on for *months*. You ask the same employee for a monthly summary of collections and receivables, and you don't have a clue that anything is missing.

Setting up controls.   How can you avoid these situations? One of the first rules is to never delegate all of the money functions to one person. Your trusted employee can stay a trusted employee if you don't leave the door open for any temptation. An easy line of demarcation is that one person can be responsible for deposit activity and another for disbursements. If the same person is responsible for both, it's easy to see how a few deposits just mysteriously disappear. Consider having two people sign all checks; this is an excellent check-and-balance system.

Second, make sure your employees know that it is a firing offense if anything is stolen. This can be anything from stealing inventory to making long-distance calls to Tahiti. Be firm on this, and establish it in writing to protect you in the unfortunate event that you need to do an immediate dismissal.

Third, remember who's the boss. That's right—it's your responsibility to pay attention to the comings and goings of your cash. Monthly reports are not acceptable. Weekly reports should be the minimum. Daily reports are appropriate if there's a lot of cash coming in and going out. Just having a frequent reporting process in place will make it more difficult for an employee to be tempted.

Background checks.   If your company is big enough that you have to hire someone as a full-time controller or treasurer, make sure that you do a background check on the person. And, yes, do the background check even if you know the person. It's what you *don't* know that can hurt you.

This due diligence is even more critical if you enter a formal partnership agreement with someone. While you may have excellent business rapport and professional synergy, you still need to investigate the person's background. Think of the horror of finding out that your new partner's personal assets have been attached by the IRS—and that the profits from your new partnership must go toward repaying that serious obligation.

Audits.   As the company grows, you'll eventually want to perform audits to verify that your actual accounts match up with what is stated on paper. An outside CPA firm can do this, or you can hire a controller to do this as part of the internal audit responsibility. A bank will also want to see audited financial statements as the company grows, so audits will indeed become part of your routine.

Insurance.   Fire or theft can leave a small business devastated. Work with an insurance broker to make sure that you have adequate coverage. Having good property and casualty insurance is a necessary investment that represents good risk management. If you're thinking that your business is too small for this, think again. Often, the smaller the business, the greater the impact of the loss.

As an aside, you'll also need to have adequate property and casualty insurance as part of every commercial lease that you sign. And if you want to borrow from a bank, they're going to want to see a copy of the policy.

An important component of a smart security system is an off-site location for storing valuable documents and data. To protect against fire, theft, or loss, a safe-deposit box at a local bank is a secure, cost-effective solution. Use it to store regular backups of customer records, bookkeeping data, and other computer files from your hard drive; copies of your insurance policies; receipts and warranties for major business purchases; photocopies of your business and personal credit cards; videotapes or photos of the contents of your office or warehouse; copies of personal identification; and stock certificates or other government documents.

Your local police. Ask your local police to check out your business location and advise you about any security precautions. One business owner we know learned about this option the hard way. After a theft occurred in her office, she called the police to file a report—a necessary part of the insurance claims process. After filing the report, the police made an excellent suggestion about a different kind of lock for the front door. This suggestion was based on how break-in crimes tended to be done in that area.

The subject of controls often leaves business owners squirming with discomfort. Yet, it's reality—and everything mentioned here happens to naive, well-meaning business owners. It often starts with the invincible feeling that nothing will get stolen; you won't have a fire; you just left your laptop for a minute at the airport. Be savvy, and get some good, basic controls in place. Doing so will eliminate much of the risk.

Chapter 38

Financial Statements— the Balance Sheet

No understanding of the language of money would be complete without an understanding of financial statements. There are three key money management tools: the *balance sheet,* the *income statement,* and the *cash-flow statement.* Each gives a particular picture of your business, and when taken together, they reveal important information about the overall financial health of your company. In this and the following two chapters, we'll show you the role each plays in monitoring your money; we'll start with the balance sheet.

In its simplest terms, the balance sheet is a snapshot of one day in time that reflects what your company owns and what it owes. The statement is often presented in two columns. On the left are the assets (what it owns); on the right side are the liabilities (what it owes) and the shareholder's equity.

The balance sheet derives its name from the fact that it is always in balance. Looking at the two columns, the basic equation is: assets (on the left) = liabilities + shareholder's equity (on the right). Another way to understand this equation is: shareholder's equity = assets − liabilities, meaning you subtract what you owe from what you own to determine your shareholder's equity. If you own more than you owe, you have a positive shareholder's equity, or net worth.

Figure 38.1 shows a sample balance sheet. Keep in mind that every balance sheet will look a little different because every business is unique. The balance sheet we've presented is for a service-type business, and in the following sections we'll review what each of the categories means.

Assets

Current assets include cash and other assets that will be converted to cash in a short time. *Cash* is essentially your bank balance. *Accounts receivable* are amounts owed by your customers that have not yet been paid. *Inventory* is divided

Figure 38.1

SAMPLE BALANCE SHEET

XYZ Company
Balance Sheet
December 31, 1998 and 1997

ASSETS	**12/31/98**	**12/31/97**
Cash	$ 19,750	$12,750
Accounts receivable	39,000	34,000
Inventory	3,000	2,500
Prepaid expenses	1,000	750
Total current assets	$ 62,750	$50,000
Property, plant, and equipment		
Computer equipment	50,000	40,000
Furniture, fixtures, etc.	5,000	4,000
Total PP&E	55,000	44,000
Less: accumulated depreciation	10,000	8,000
Net PP&E	45,000	36,000
Total assets	$107,750	$86,000
LIABILITIES	**12/31/98**	**12/31/97**
Accounts payable	$ 15,000	$12,500
Notes payable	2,750	5,250
Accrued expenses	7,500	6,000
Income taxes payable	4,250	3,750
Total current liabilities	$ 29,500	$27,500
Long-term debt	12,250	2,250
Total liabilities	$ 41,750	$29,750
Shareholder's Equity		
Common stock	50,000	50,000
Retained earnings	16,000	6,250
Total SE	$ 66,000	$56,250
Total liabilities + SE	$107,750	$86,000

into three categories: *raw materials,* which are what goes into making your product; *work in process,* which are partially completed goods; and *finished goods,* which are products ready for shipment. If you have a service business where you're selling your time, the inventory amount will be inconsequential. (You'll note that in Figure 38.1, our balance sheet for a service business, we have a modest amount for inventory.) Finally, *prepaid expenses* are anything you have paid for in advance. This would include something like prepaid utilities or insurance policies. *Total current assets* is a number used in most liquidity ratios.

The next asset category is *property, plant, and equipment* (PP&E). These are assets that are *used* by the company and are not intended for sale. Examples are furniture, equipment, land, buildings, and cars. As these are assets that wear out over time, their value is reduced every year by a predetermined amount of money called *depreciation.* The amount of PP&E on the balance sheet is reduced by the amount of accumulated depreciation for those assets.

Intangibles are assets that do not have physical properties, such as trademarks, patents, and goodwill. If your business has an exclusive feature, such as a proprietary client list or a brand identity, that would be considered an intangible. Intangibles are very difficult to value and are difficult to document (which is why you won't find any listed on our sample in Figure 38.1). If your business has assets of intangible value, your CPA can help you attach a figure to them and incorporate them into your balance sheet.

Liabilities and Shareholder's Equity

Current liabilities represent all debts that will be paid within a year. Remember current assets? It's the cash generated from current assets that will be used to pay down your current liabilities. *Accounts payable* are amounts you owe to suppliers and vendors. *Notes payable*—or loans payable—are the principal amounts due on loans that are less than one year old (for example, amounts due under your line of credit or the current portion of long-term debt). *Accrued liabilities* are any other amounts owed in the short-term—salaries, fees for professional services, your pension fund, and so forth. *Taxes payable* are all the taxes you owe in the given period. Total current liabilities are the sum of all of these items.

The rest of a company's liabilities are its *long-term liabilities*—these are amounts due on term loans or deferred income taxes (which are tax incentives available to certain types of industries).

The *shareholder's equity* account shows the value of your *capital stock,* if any, and *retained earnings.* Retained earnings represent the cumulative net income of your company.

Balance Sheet Analysis

Now that you have all the numbers on your balance sheet, let's take a look at what they mean. Current assets less current liabilities is called *working capital.* Of course, this number should be a positive one—the question is, to what degree? When you divide current assets by current liabilities, the resulting *current ratio* is a liquidity measure frequently used by investors. It shows how many times the current debt could be paid off with the current assets. If the ratio is 2 to 1 or higher, it's generally viewed favorably by banks. In this case, the current ratio is 2.13 to 1 in 1998, having improved from 1.82 to 1 in 1997.

This ratio can tell us several things. If the ratio is too low, it's a sign that the business may be short of cash and won't be able to pay suppliers. In contrast, if the ratio is too high, it could mean that assets aren't being used in a productive way. Keep in mind, though, that you should check your ratios against those that are the standard for your industry. (See Chapter 31 for more details on ratios and industry standards.)

Ratios *are pairings of numbers that show a relationship between the two numbers. Financial ratios can seem confusing at first, but don't be intimidated. You probably use a ratio frequently when evaluating automobile fuel efficiency—yes, miles per gallon. There are a variety of ratios that financial professionals use, and each tells a different story. What they're doing is looking at the relationship between two different aspects of your business finances, and comparing them to established benchmarks to see how strong your business is.*

An asset-based lender or factor will spend considerable time measuring how quickly your inventory turns into receivables, and how quickly your receivables are collected. For this reason, you'll probably need to prepare monthly balance sheets for their review.

The balance sheet also measures a company's *debt capacity.* Lenders don't want to advance you more debt than you can handle. To determine your debt capacity, a lender will use a benchmark of the *debt-to-equity ratio,* which is total debt divided by shareholder's equity. If this ratio is higher than 2 to 1, lenders will take a closer look at your credit capacity. Our company enjoys a low 0.23-to-1 debt-to-equity ratio, allowing room for the addition of debt when the appropriate opportunity presents itself.

You can see by the nature of assets and liabilities that a balance sheet changes from one day to the next. Balance sheets are always dated on the particular date chosen, usually year-end or quarter-end. Investors will compare data on a year-to-year basis to see how the asset and liability categories are shifting as the company grows. If your business has a seasonal element, this is also captured in the balance sheet. For example, a retail business that makes a lot of sales in December might have high levels of inventory buildup beginning in October. This will affect the company's working capital to the point where it may need to borrow under a line of credit until the inventory is sold off.

As a business owner, what does a balance sheet tell you? It shows how liquid the company is and how much debt it is using. It also shows if there are enough short-term assets to cover short-term liabilities. Both of these elements are important factors for you to know in managing your business—and it is essential to keep them in line if you want to secure financing from outside lenders.

Fortunately, accounting software can easily generate your company's balance sheet. We encourage you to learn to monitor it the same way a lender does. It's a valuable way to learn to anticipate working capital shifts and changes in your company's debt capacity.

Chapter 39

Financial Statements— the Income Statement

W hile the balance sheet talks about what you own and what you owe, the income statement tells you what you've sold and what you've spent. An income statement reflects the profit and loss of the company, and is sometimes referred to as the *profit and loss* (P&L) statement. It measures sales or revenues minus all expenses and taxes and shows the *bottom line* for the company—how much money it has made.

Income statements show how a company performs over a specific period of time, usually a month, a quarter, or a year. You'll find a sample income statement in Figure 39.1. Let's take a look at what each category means.

Income Statement Components

Revenue, or *net sales,* is the amount of money received by your company in exchange for selling products or rendering services to your customers. *Net* refers to the fact that sometimes there are refunds or returns. Many times small business owners in service businesses refer to their revenue as "gross income." Start thinking of it as revenue, because the use of the word *income* can be confusing, as you will soon see.

The *cost of goods sold* is the first expense item deducted from revenue. It refers to all of the costs that are incurred making the product that you sell. This includes direct labor, direct materials, and manufacturing overhead. Again, a service business will look different. Our example in Figure 39.1 reflects a service-type business, so in this case the direct labor would be the only real component of cost of goods sold.

The *gross profit* is what remains after you subtract the cost of goods sold from net sales. The next items to be deducted are *depreciation* and *amortization*. Depreciation reflects the decline in value of a tangible asset due to normal usage. For

Figure 39.1

INCOME STATEMENT

XYZ Company
Income Statement
For the years ended 12/31/98 and 12/31/97

	1998	1997
Net sales	$191,250	$168,500
Cost of goods sold	133,750	116,250
Gross profit	57,500	52,250
Operating expenses		
Depreciation	2,000	1,500
Selling, general, and administrative expenses	39,300	38,800
Operating income	16,200	11,950
Less: interest expense	1,200	500
Income before taxes	15,000	11,450
Income taxes	5,250	4,000
Net income	$ 9,750	$ 7,450

example, computers may be valued on a three-year life, and you would deduct one-third of its value every year as depreciation. If you own a printing press, it would be depreciated over a much longer period, such as 20 years, reflecting its longer time in use. Amortization is the decline in value of an intangible asset, such as a trademark or patent. Our example business has no intangible assets, so you won't find any amortization in Figure 39.1.

Selling, general, and administrative expenses (SG&A) reflect all expenses related to marketing, sales, promotion, and advertising, as well as general office expenses and overhead. These expenses are separated from those in cost of goods sold so you can see the difference between what is essential in making the product as opposed to selling it.

If you are the CEO of a small service business, and you are the primary revenue generator, you will allocate some of your salary to cost of goods sold—the direct labor component—and the rest will be allocated as executive salary under SG&A.

Operating income is what remains after deducting cost of goods sold, depreciation, and SG&A from sales. *Interest expense*—the interest component on any loans outstanding—is deducted next, resulting in *income before taxes.* This is the amount of income on which your company must pay federal, state, and local taxes.

A *provision for taxes* is then deducted, based on the statutory amounts. The resulting *net income* is the income generated after all costs and expenses are deducted.

Analysis

As with the balance sheet, a year-to-year or quarter-to-quarter comparison tells more than does just looking at the numbers in isolation. *Margin analysis* will evaluate how much money is being kept for every dollar of sales. *Gross margin,* the gross profit divided by sales, is evaluated very closely in retail businesses. This will pick up the ability of a retailer to move inventory at a reasonable speed. The gross margin is also important in manufacturing companies, as it reflects how efficiently raw materials are converted into sold product.

The *operating margin,* or operating income divided by sales, shows how much money is being made from the basic operations of the company. If this ratio improves from year to year, it reflects an improvement in the overall operating performance of the company. In this example, the operating margin improved from 7.1 percent in 1997 to 8.5 percent in 1998.

Sometimes small businesses will be aggressive with expenses in order to keep a lower level of income before taxes. This is a legitimate strategy where the business owner is only trying to reduce his or her company's tax liability. The flip side of this, though, is that a lender may think that the expenses are too high to afford the loan you may be requesting. Small business lenders should understand this dynamic, but you may need to drive home the point if you are working with an inexperienced account officer who may be less familiar with the small business mentality.

Another area of income statement analysis always examined by lenders is *interest coverage* (how much operating profit a company has available to pay its interest expenses). Lenders are conservative by nature, and they want to know how well a company can pay its interest expenses. One of the commonly used ratios is *earnings before interest and taxes* (operating income in this case), divided by interest expense. Earnings before interest and taxes is commonly referred to as *EBIT* (pronounced *ee-bit*). Another way to look at this is earnings before interest and taxes plus depreciation and amortization (EBITDA) divided by interest expense. This variation adds back depreciation and amortization because, while they are deducted on the income statement, they are not cash charges. Our company's EBIT ratio is a strong 13.5× in 1998, reflecting its low level of debt. Not only does this company have the capacity to increase debt (discussed in the last chapter), but it also has the ability to comfortably handle additional interest coverage.

All companies will be evaluated somewhat differently on these ratios. Interest coverage is critical, though, when loans are being made to your company. If your EBIT is only two to three times your projected interest expense, the banks will be leery about lending. This is because a drop in sales means you'll have less profit, and you may then be in trouble paying your interest expense. Essentially, the banks want to be sure that if there's a decline in your business, they'll still get paid. We recommend that you ask your banker for a good interest coverage benchmark for your business, and start monitoring it on a regular basis.

The net income figure is added to retained earnings at the end of the period. This is where the company's earnings and balance sheets intersect. The higher the level of income, the more that is added to retained earnings. This increases the overall value of the company.

If your company is publicly held, the analysis will extend to *earnings per share* (net income divided by the number of shares of common stock outstanding) and the *price to earnings ratio* (the market price of the stock divided by earnings per share). These are two measures that are carefully scrutinized by anyone investing in your stock. If the P/E ratio is too high for the industry, for example, it suggests that the market price of your stock is overvalued, and it's a signal that it may drop. While earnings per share and P/E multiples are far beyond most small businesses, it's always interesting to see what major corporations are facing—and what you need to worry about when thinking of greener grass.

Chapter 40

Financial Statements— the Cash Flow Statement

B y now you've learned that a balance sheet reflects what you own and owe; an income statement shows what you sold and spent. We now come to the third important financial management tool—the statement of cash flow— which ties the two together.

In financial statement analysis, the balance sheet and income statements get a lot of coverage, while the statement of cash flow is often ignored. We think that's a big mistake, since cash-flow management is what keeps some companies in business when others just can't make it.

In Figure 40.1, you'll find an example statement of cash flow for a service business. Let's explore what it tells us.

The statement of cash flow reconciles the change in the cash account from one period to another. For example, the cash account of XYZ Company increased from $12,750 at year-end 1997 to $19,750 at year-end 1998. At the same time, net income rose and the financial ratios improved. We need to examine the changes in a variety of places to determine what really happened to that cash.

The statement of cash flow begins with net income and then makes adjustments from three categories: *operations, investing activities* (typically capital investments), and *financing activities* (such as long-term borrowings and stock issuance).

You'll note that the first item listed after net income is *depreciation*. This is added back to net income because it is a noncash charge that had been deducted from net income on the income statement. The next items are the increase or decrease (bracketed amounts) in the components of working capital, that is, current assets and current liabilities (except notes payable, which are not considered as part of cash flow from *operations*).

After all of these items are added together, the subtotal is called *net cash from operations.* This means that $750 was generated from the operating activity of the

Figure 40.1

STATEMENT OF CASH FLOW

XYZ Company
Statement of Cash Flow
For the year ended 12/31/98

Net income	$ 9,750
Cash flow from operations	
Depreciation	2,000
Increase in accounts receivable	(5,000)
Increase in inventory	(500)
Increase in prepaid expenses	(250)
Increase in accounts payable	2,500
Increase in accrued expenses	1,500
Increase in income taxes payable	500
Total from operations	$ 750
Cash flow from investing activities	
Purchase of fixed assets	(11,000)
Cash flow from financing activities	
Decrease in notes payable	(2,500)
Increase in long-term debt	10,000
Increase in cash	$ 7,000
Cash at beginning of the year	$12,750
Cash at the end of the year	$19,750

company. The next item is net cash used to purchase equipment, which is considered an *investing activity* of the company. If you bought a state-of-the-art telephone system, it cost you money, but it was an investment in your business. The reverse accounting occurs if you sold assets during the year. For example, the net cash received from the sale of a building would be added to cash from investing activities.

Finally, the cash-flow statement evaluates changes in cash flow pertaining to *financing activities*. This is where you would show the increase or decrease in loans payable, the increase or decrease in long-term debt, the issuance of stock, and the payment of dividends.

After netting the cash flow from operations, investing activities, and financing activities, you will have either a positive number, reflecting an *increase in cash,* or a negative number, showing a *decrease in cash.* This amount should match the difference in cash on the balance sheet for the periods covered.

Analysis

The cash-flow statement breaks down everything that happened during the period and shows where cash was generated and where it was used. Monitoring this statement will help you benchmark everything from a slowdown in collection of receivables to inventory turnover to investment in capital equipment.

For most small businesses, the cash-flow cycle centers around working capital. This reflects the operating cycle of the business—the cycle of cash conversion from inventory to sales to receivables to cash again.

Cash-Flow Strategies

The amount of cash on hand (the amount in your bank account) should be sufficient to cover day-to-day needs and at least one month of current liabilities. If you don't have that amount of cash, your business will get caught in a hand-to-mouth spiral that leaves the owner with the feeling of never being caught up. Here are some things you can do to tighten up your cash conversion cycle:

✓ *At the most basic level, track your receivables.*   Be aware of what payments are due to you, and when.

✓ *Collect sooner from your customers.*   There is no reason they cannot pay sooner. State your payment terms clearly on your invoices, and bring in cash earlier than you have been.

✓ *Don't load up on inventory.*   It eats cash and you can't get it back until you make more sales.

✓ *Stretch your payables without hurting your vendors.*   If you have established 30-day trade credit, take full advantage of the 30 days—but don't be late. You want to maintain excellent trade credit.

✓ *Evaluate your marketing strategy.*   If you're strapped for cash, you may want to do business that brings in more cash on a short-term basis and save longer-term projects for when you are not juggling cash.

Savvy business owners know where their cash is. They do cash-flow budgeting and track the actual numbers on a regular basis (at least monthly, often more frequently if the business has large cash turnover). If you're not familiar with your company's cash flow, it's time to become so. You'll find that when you devote more time to cash-flow analysis, you'll make better projections, which will create a positive ripple effect through every part of your business.

Chapter 41

Budgeting Strategies

Virtually every small business owner plays the cash-juggling game. Unfortunately, sometimes the game doesn't quite hold up, and we're left in an embarrassing, frustrating, or even financially risky situation. What's the solution? Defining a structure and working within it—in other words, *budgeting*.

Budgeting provides a sensible, proactive way to diminish the gaps that can come from guessing your cash position. Once you set up a budget, you'll be able to track your results as frequently as you want, and retain better control of your business.

There are many types of budgets, for many reasons. For example, if you're working on a special project, you might set up a project budget that defines the income and expenses involved in it. Lenders will likely want to see a budget for the overall operations of your business, and how close you are to meeting your projections. In this chapter, however, we'll focus on a *cash-flow budget,* since we feel it is one of the most critical ingredients to your company's success.

Process. Budgeting should be an annual process with frequent reviews throughout the year. When your business is in a growth mode, it's best to review it on a monthly basis at a minimum. If you're aggressively managing cash flow, you may want to make it a weekly examination. The easiest way to manage a budget is by using spreadsheet software. That way it will be easy to change assumptions and recalculate your results.

When performing the annual budget ritual, it's a good idea to go through your prior year's statements line by line to determine if you're spending too much or too little in each of the accounts. You may have been bootstrapping in prior years, for example, and can now afford to invest more in promotional expense. Or, you may see that your inventory turns are too slow, so you can decide to reduce your inventory purchases until the old inventory runs down.

Gather all of your data before beginning. A good way to get a handle on cash-flow forecasting is to study your historical pattern. If you have maintained accurate records, you should be able to reproduce a monthly statement using the categories that follow. Once you have analyzed your pattern, you can break down the operating numbers as follows:

✓ *Sales forecast.* These are your projected monthly sales, taking into account any cyclicality. If you have different product areas, you may want to split this forecast into those categories.

✓ *Monthly fixed expenses.* These are expenses that you pay every month, whether you're selling a lot or a little. These include items such as rent, utilities, and payroll.

✓ *Monthly variable expenses.* These are expenses whose amounts vary monthly, depending on the volume of sales. These include SG&A items, such as phone, travel and entertainment, advertising, legal and accounting, maintenance and cleaning, postage, courier and delivery, office expenses, supplies, collections, depreciation, and so forth.

In addition to regular operations, however, you may have some one-time capital or project expenditures that you will want to include:

✓ *Purchase of capital equipment.* This includes your investment in new equipment, such as a copier, fax machine, or other item.

✓ *Project planning.* This includes any big-ticket expenses for the upcoming year (for example, new logo design or the launch of a new product).

Evaluate all large expenditures with a critical eye to make sure that you'll be receiving an appropriate return on investment. Don't hold back if you need to make the investment in a big-ticket item to grow the business. Not investing can be as detrimental as spending money irresponsibly. If you don't know how to evaluate return on investment, ask your banker or accountant for assistance. They can walk you through the process and help you analyze your options.

The last item you need is the opening bank balance for the initial period (or the closing bank balance for the previous period—it will be the same figure). This amount will be your opening cash position in the forecast. Using the example, the company ended the year with a balance of $19,750, which also represents the opening cash position for January 1, 1999.

Once you have identified these amounts, adapt the template in Figure 41.1 into a spreadsheet format. You can then insert the amounts for each month, and in a short time you'll have your cash needs projected for the year.

One of the key features of this forecast is the use of sales actually collected, which we are calling *cash sales*. To properly budget this number, you'll need to

Figure 41.1

CASH-FLOW FORECAST

	January	February
Sales		
Cash received	$15,000	14,000
Accounts receivable	9,000	9,500
Expenses		
Inventory	100	100
Equipment	0	5,000
Salaries	4,000	4,000
Rent	1,500	1,500
Utilities	150	150
Phone	350	350
Internet	30	30
Insurance	200	200
Legal/accounting	1,000	0
Travel/entertainment	1,200	1,200
Selling expenses	500	500
Advertising	0	0
Maintenance/cleaning	100	100
Courier/delivery	250	250
Office expense	300	300
Books/periodicals	100	100
Dues/professional memberships	0	200
Supplies	50	50
Collections	0	0
Loans	0	0
Income taxes	400	400
Payroll taxes	100	100
Other	0	0
Total expenses	$10,330	$14,530
Net cash flow	4,670	(530)
Cumulative cash flow	4,670	4,140
Reconciliation		
Opening Cash	19,750	24,420
+Cash receipts	15,000	14,000
−Cash disbursements	(10,330)	(14,530)
Closing cash balance	$24,420	$23,890

(Continued) ⟹

This chart represents a two-month sample of a company's budget. As you can see from this example, some expenses—such as rent, salaries, and utilities—are fairly easy to budget evenly throughout the year. In other cases, such as legal and accounting services or the purchase of equipment, the expenses are budgeted in the month in which they are expected to be paid.

know the average number of days it takes you to collect payment from your customers, also known as *days sales outstanding*. For example, if it takes an average of 30 days for you to receive payment from your customers, you'll record that amount in the following month, not the current month. This reflects that you'll be receiving the payment 30 days from now, which gives you a more realistic tool for managing your cash.

If you have a manufacturing or retail business, you'll also need to know your historical *gross profit margin* to budget your cost of goods sold.

After your budget is in place, don't shove it in some back drawer or abandon it on your hard drive and forget about it. This cash-flow plan is a living, active document that will be one of your best management tools. Study it regularly and compare your actual monthly results with the budgeted amounts to see where you over- or underestimated. Doing this habitually will help you understand the rhythm of your cash flow, and you'll find yourself getting better at the process as years go by.

Not quite convinced? Yes, there are many benefits to the budget process. First, you're able to predict when you'll have cash shortfalls. Knowing that in advance helps you decide whether you'll borrow under your line of credit or delay a payment. Whichever the decision, it sure beats overdrawing your account and incurring embarrassment, credit penalties, and fees. Second, you can plan larger expenditures around periods when you know you'll be receiving more cash. Third, you can manage your line of credit borrowings better, which will inevitably result in lower interest expense. Finally, your banker will have a greater appreciation for you when he or she sees that you understand the critical role of cash flow.

When your business experiences a growth spurt, you'll need more cash than in periods of regular growth. In that case, you'll need to borrow more often to balance the mismatching of cash inflows and outflows. You can always tell business owners who are cash-flow oriented—they can tell you what they have in the bank within a small margin of error. They know exactly how their money is working for them. Any business owner can learn this; it just takes focused, consistent effort.

Chapter 42

Financial Partners—Your Banker

If there's one piece of advice we could give every business owner, this would be it: Establishing a strong relationship with your banker is one of the most important steps you can take to build a successful business.

Savvy entrepreneurs take steps to create alliances with bankers, regardless of whether their banking needs are as modest as a checking account or involve more sophisticated financing arrangements. These smart business owners know that building these relationships should be done steadily, over time. Creating a sense of rapport and communication when you really don't need financing can pay off when you do need it. Here's how you can build and cement a better relationship with your banker.

Branch manager.   Introduce yourself to the manager at the branch where your account is located. If your account is not in a convenient location, it's worth the effort to move it to a branch where you have ready access to the branch manager. Also, take copies of some of your promotional materials, such as brochures, sales sheets, or press clippings as a way for him or her to get a sense of your business.

Share a copy of your business plan.   Send your plan to the branch manager and follow up with a meeting where you can articulate your vision and goals for the business. This is your opportunity to showcase your business and establish your image as the owner/CEO of your company. By knowing more about who you are and what you do, your banker may be more comfortable referring you to possible clients, vendors, or business partners.

Make contact with your banker once a quarter.   Make consistent contact with your banker so that he or she will recognize you when you call. For example, drop a note with a press clipping or a short description of a new business opportunity you've developed. Another idea is to send a copy of a testimonial letter from a client. If you're speaking before any civic groups or business associations, extend a personal invitation to the banker to attend.

If your business takes you traveling to unusual destinations, consider sending postcards to your banker. Why? Because the bankers enjoy knowing of your success—and the recognition you give them for being part of it. For example, when Terri gave a keynote speech in Tokyo, she sent postcards to several members of her professional advisory team, including her banker. He enjoyed the remembrance, and it helped secure their professional relationship.

Review your financial statements with your banker. If the bank is lending you money, you already know how frequently it expects updated financial statements. If you don't yet have a credit relationship, submit an income statement, balance sheet, and cash-flow statement at least once a year. Not only does this help build the relationship, it also demonstrates that you're fiscally responsible.

Ask for advice. Bankers can be valuable resources. They usually have experience with many types of clients, and they may have just the answer to a challenge you're facing. They also can provide a perspective on industry trends or comparable financial performance ratios of others in your industry. Bankers can also advise you on financial management tactics as your company grows. This may include advice on when you need to have financial statements audited by a CPA.

Know what you want. Understand what a banker is willing to invest in you. If you're working with a large bank, the telephone may be your primary means of contact. The account officers in these banks are not going to devote the time to a relationship that a community banker will. You can still cultivate a relationship with someone in a large bank, but it will be more difficult. They'll rely on credit scoring to lend you money, and you can expect frequent account officer turnover.

If regular, personal contact is important to you, you'll probably be better off working with a community bank than a large multinational one. You can always grow into a larger bank after getting established with a smaller one.

Make sure there's depth in your contacts. As your needs grow, be sure you cultivate a relationship with more than one person at your bank. In this era of merger mania with banks consolidating, downsizing, and reorganizing, you never know when your account officer may be reassigned or laid off. It's every small business owner's nightmare these days: spending months or years to develop a relationship with a banker, and bingo, that person is gone. Get to know others to protect your interests.

When you're a borrower.   After you begin borrowing from a bank, you'll take the relationship to the next level. First, view your banker as a key ex officio member of your management team. Use his or her expertise to build your business. Solicit candid opinions about your business and industry. Ask for introductions to potential clients, vendors, or outside professionals. *Never* let your banker find out bad news about your business through the grapevine. Painful as it may be, if the business has a problem, get on the phone before someone else does.

Banker wish list.   Bankers are eager to do business; they also know how small business owners can be good customers. Here's what bankers have told us:

✓   Small business owners need to recognize their company's weaknesses and be *willing and prepared to address them.*

✓   Learn to be a good listener. Don't judge *what* you are hearing; instead, pay attention and ask questions. Many entrepreneurs are not good listeners, and it's frustrating for bankers to deal with customers with short attention spans.

✓   Small business owners need to learn how to validate what they learn from a banker. Do yourself and the business the favor of verifying what you've learned by talking to another banker.

Know the decision maker.   Today it seems as if there is unlimited money available for small business loans. Part of this perception is based on the fact that many of the people who solicit small business customers are business development professionals. Their job is to sell—they prequalify customers, and once this is done, they pass the prospective customer to the credit officers. Upon meeting someone who seems interested in your business, find out if they're an account officer who has credit authority or a business development expert. This one piece of information can save you a lot of time.

There are those who feel that there is a natural animosity between small business owners and bankers. This is a foolish generalization, and one you can avoid by being proactive in establishing rapport from an early stage of your business. Don't wait until you need to borrow money to meet your banker. Rather, be known to him or her from an early stage. By building this relationship, you become a known quantity to the bank in both good and bad times. As a result of your efforts, you'll reap the dividends for many years to come.

Chapter 43

Financial Partners— Accounting Professionals

But I don't need an accountant. . . ." These words are naively spoken by many business owners. If you're serious about being in business, you must engage an accountant. This person can help your business in so many different ways, that *not* to use one is a disservice. Accountants, bookkeepers, and controllers are all accounting professionals who can play different roles to help your business grow.

Distinctions. Many people use the expressions *accountant* and *CPA* interchangeably. They are not the same. CPAs are more likely to advise you about general business issues, whereas accountants are usually qualified only to prepare your tax returns.

There is no uniformity in the background of *accountants.* Some have substantial technical training, others may have taken one course. There are no national licensing requirements or exams, so it's difficult to evaluate an accountant on the basis of education and training. There may be the perception that accountants charge less than CPAs, which is not always true. A number of small business owners will select an accountant based on price. This can be foolish economy.

A *CPA,* or *certified public accountant,* receives this designation after passing a two-day national examination. In addition, CPAs must meet experience requirements prior to being licensed by the state in which they operate. CPAs can be members of the American Institute of Certified Public Accountants (AICPA).

Working with a CPA. As soon as it makes sense, hire a CPA. He or she will be an extended member of your management team, and can help you work through some of the growing pains in your business. A CPA can assist in a variety of small business accounting and auditing functions:

✓ Performing an audit or preparing financial statements

✓ Reviewing forecasts or financial projections

✓ Developing formats for regular monthly or quarterly reporting

✓ Analyzing your company's operating results

✓ Advising you on the selection and use of computer software

✓ Referring you to qualified bookkeepers or other outsourced services

In addition, CPAs can consult on a broad range of financial issues, ranging from cash management to business valuation to compliance with governmental regulations. They can assist with inventory management, financial analysis, and pricing strategies as well.

The American Institute of Certified Public Accountants (AICPA) is the leading national association for CPAs in the United States. An organization of more than 330,000 members, it has strict professional, technical, and ethical requirements that its members must uphold. The AICPA Web site (http://www.aicpa.org) features information to help small business owners understand the value of working with a CPA, tips on how to work with them, and suggestions on how to find one in your area. The site also features links to a broad list of accounting-related sites. To contact the AICPA offices, call (212) 596-6200.

CPAs can prepare your income tax returns, advise you about the implications of tax law changes on your business, and suggest strategies for tax savings. A CPA can also advise you on the financial impact of the legal structure of your company. (You may want to speak with both your CPA and attorney on this legal matter.)

How to select a CPA.   Like any other professional, CPAs' qualifications and experience vary. You will want to interview several CPAs to determine which one is the best fit for your company. If you hire someone and find that it is not working out, you are entirely within your rights to fire that person and move on. You may go through several CPAs before you find the one that is right for your business.

Start by networking with other business owners for referrals to CPAs. Also ask your banker or attorney; they have a vested interest in working with the best CPAs. Chances are, you'll be able to find one through your professional contacts in your community, but if you have difficulty, contact the state's society of CPAs for referrals.

Here are some questions you may want to ask during the interview process:

✓ What types of businesses do you work with? Have you worked with companies in my industry?

✓　Do you do the actual work yourself, or will you be delegating it to another person?

✓　Do you take an aggressive or conservative stance on expense items?

✓　What do you do in the event of an audit? Will you represent my company if we have to meet with the IRS or local authorities?

✓　Are you licensed in this state?

✓　How do you charge (hourly or retainer)? What are your fees?

✓　What kind of accounting software do you recommend? Will you help me get started on the software?

Ongoing relationship.　The key to a good partnership with your CPA is to have regular contact. You should meet at least quarterly for business updates. If you only visit your CPA once a year at tax time, you are not maximizing your relationship.

Other accounting professionals.　If you're seeking a tax specialist for your business, investigate whether there are any enrolled agents (EAs) in your area. These financial professionals must take a two-day comprehensive national exam given by the IRS. As licensed tax experts, EAs, along with CPAs and tax attorneys, are among the few tax professionals who can represent taxpayers before the IRS without the taxpayer being present. Although some EAs do bookkeeping and accounting work, most are not accountants. If your accountant or CPA is not interested in or qualified for preparing tax returns, check out an enrolled agent for the peace of mind of knowing your taxes are being prepared by a licensed professional.

As your business grows, it will be necessary to hire part-time or full-time people to handle the financial functions. Your CPA should be able to refer other professionals to you. In most cases, these would be bookkeepers or controllers. In Chapter 36, we covered some of the ways in which a *bookkeeper* can help your business run more smoothly. You may be able to expand the scope of your bookkeeper's responsibilities, depending on that person's experience and background.

When the business reaches a certain critical mass, you may consider hiring a *controller.* This person serves as an in-house accountant, conducts operational and financial analysis, and will supervise the bookkeeping function and communicate with your CPA. The controller takes a bigger picture view of controls, systems, and forecasting for the firm.

If your company is looking to do a public offering, merger, or acquisition, you may want to hire a *freelance chief financial officer.* This outsourced person would work closely with you on all tactical issues and decisions pertaining to the big event. It would free you to focus more on the strategic issues, rather than the details of writing an offering memorandum or conducting preliminary interviews with investment banks or brokers. By working with a freelance professional, you will not pay the steep price of a full-time CFO. Alternatively, you may want to put an outsourced CFO on retainer to your company.

Throughout this book, we've used the term *accountant* for ease of writing. We strongly recommend, however, that you select a CPA as a financial partner for your business. This is particularly important if you're going to be borrowing from a bank or raising money in some other venue. Bankers are serious about financial obligations, and they will view a CPA more favorably than an accountant. Remember, your business is more than an accumulation of numbers. You want someone with deep financial knowledge and experience to help you translate those numbers into meaningful tools to help you grow your business.

Chapter 44

Financial Partners—
Insurance Brokers

The subject of insurance is one that many small business owners avoid—mainly due to lack of understanding of what insurance can do for you and your business. Very briefly, you buy insurance to decrease your business risk and to gain the security that comes from protecting your assets. The key to achieving this security is finding an excellent insurance broker. He or she should be someone you trust, because you'll be making many decisions on things that can have a significant bottom-line impact on your business.

The old way. Most small business owners have their first taste of the insurance world because they have to. You have to get property and casualty insurance as a condition for your commercial lease. Or, you have to get health insurance. Bring up the subject of insurance and most small business owners' eyes glaze over.

The proactive approach. Let your broker know what your expectations are. Discuss them so each of you knows what level of service is appropriate. Think of your broker as an outsourced risk-management partner.

The many-businesses approach. Start approaching the insurance equation from a strategic perspective. Understand that insurance is really many businesses. There is property and casualty, liability, life, workers' compensation, health, disability, long-term care—and many more esoteric subdivisions. Insurance *decreases* your risk, protecting you and your business from catastrophic events that could wipe out all of your assets or earnings. When you think of it this way, it seems a less bothersome overhead expense.

Property and casualty insurance.   This protects you from fire and theft on your premises. Think of it as covering everything from the walls in: your furniture, equipment, artwork, carpeting, and any leasehold improvements. Buy this insurance for *replacement* coverage. Consider this: If everything was damaged in a fire, how much would it cost to replace everything that you lost? Probably much more in today's dollars than you originally paid for it.

Liability insurance.   You need this coverage to protect you if anyone hurts himself on your premises or in your vehicles. For example, if a customer slips and breaks a leg, this would be covered under your liability policy. Another variation of liability insurance is director and officers' (D&O) insurance, which you may get for your corporate officers and members of your board of directors.

Aon Enterprise Insurance Services represents a consortium of leading insurance companies (including Chubb Group, Kemper, and Wausau insurance companies) that offers a one-stop-shopping approach to insurance and other financial services designed specifically for small business owners. For more information, call their toll-free Technology Center hotline for small business customers at (888) 781-3272, or visit the Aon Web site at http//www.aonenterprise.com.

Life insurance.   Life insurance is a risk-management vehicle that can enhance the value of your estate, send your children to college, provide income for your family, pay off your creditors, and provide cash so that you can be assured that your business continuation plans will be completed.

It's wise to use the advice and guidance of a life insurance professional to make sure that the insurance is structured properly. By so doing, you'll know that the right person gets the right amount of proceeds at the right time. Legal agreements (wills, trusts, buy-sell agreements, separation agreements, and so forth) are normally needed in addition to the life insurance policy. Your agent can help you coordinate the insurance with your other advisors, and often he or she can orchestrate the entire process.

Many people wonder which life insurance product is most appropriate. Generally, if the need for the coverage is less than eight years, term insurance would normally be the appropriate recommendation. On the other hand, in many buy-sell situations, estate planning, and personal planning, a permanent form of insurance may be needed. A good insurance agent will be able to help you understand your objectives and will review the advantages of each approach.

Many Internet Web sites feature information and interactive tools to help you calculate the ideal amount or type of coverage that meets your needs. For example, Insurance News Network (http://www.insure.com) is an independently owned and operated publisher of insurance information, which it makes available free on the Web. Quotesmith (http://www.quotesmith.com) operates the largest insurance information database in America. At this writing, it tracks the rates and coverage of about 350 leading insurance companies in a continually updated database.

Disability insurance. Once you are in your twenties, the odds are much greater that you may suffer a disability than that you'll die. However, the results are often nearly as grim: Your earning ability can abruptly stop. To offset this risk, disability insurance replaces a percentage of your income while you're unable to work. You can get personal disability coverage—which would take care of your household and living expenses—as well as business disability coverage. This covers your basic business overhead expenses if you become disabled.

Health insurance. This coverage can consume a large portion of your budget for insurance. Evaluate coverage based on the number of people you need to cover—whether it's just you or a staff of 20. Health insurance from your trade association or local chamber of commerce is often a good option for small business owners, because they can negotiate lower premium rates for group coverage.

State requirements. *Workers' compensation insurance* is required coverage by law for all employees. This varies on a state-by-state basis, but will need to be paid at least quarterly by most small business owners. Virtually every state requires payment of *short-term disability* as well. Talk to your insurance broker about your requirements.

Long-term care. This coverage protects your assets if you have to go into a nursing home or use the services of a home health care institution. While it does not have a direct impact on your business, you may want to plan for it as part of your overall financial planning strategy.

Small business strategies. Decide how much money you want to budget for insurance and then work with your insurance broker to establish priorities. Examine the different levels of cost based on different deductibles. Taking a higher deductible results in a lower premium expense, but at some point, the deductible will be too high. Work through the analysis with your insurance broker.

Most insurance brokers have a network of specialists, so you may have a broker who specializes in life insurance, and he or she will refer you to someone else who handles property and casualty. When working with a broker, consider these issues:

✓ Ask about the rating of the insurance company underwriting your coverage. The rating tells you about the company's claims-paying ability. You don't want to buy coverage and not be able to receive the cash from a claim.

✓ You'll want to know about the kind of service you will receive from your broker. Ask about customer service issues, such as how soon your calls will be returned, reporting procedures, and so forth.

✓ When you make changes in your business, talk to your broker to see if you need to make any adjustments to your coverage.

✓ If you're a home-based business, make sure that the broker understands those unique issues. At this writing, the insurance industry still doesn't know how to uniformly respond to home-based business issues. Several companies have created packages that piggyback business insurance with homeowner's coverage, but there are a number of gray areas that have not been fully resolved, such as liability issues. Do your homework to find the representative in your area who knows home-based businesses best.

We hope this overview has convinced you of the important role a good insurance broker can play in your business. You can find top-notch professionals through the usual networking venues—your Chamber of Commerce, other business owners, your trade associations, and other members of your professional advisory team. Insurance is largely a business of referrals, so ask around and interview a few different people until you find someone who is knowledgeable and willing to work with the amount of money you have to invest.

Chapter 45

Financial Partners—Attorneys

You may have looked at this chapter title and wondered how attorneys could be your *financial* partners. That's easy—if you have the right kind of attorneys on your team, over time you will save large amounts of money. It's a twist on the classic adage, "It takes money to make money."

General practitioner. Finding the right attorney for your business is a godsend. A good general business attorney will be able to address most of the day-to-day needs of your business. For example, most businesses engage in some types of contracts. Your attorney will be able to review these and help you negotiate terms that are most advantageous for the company.

In addition, you may need to have leases reviewed. From commercial leases for rental property to equipment leases when making capital investments, there is a lot of legalese that your attorney can manage on your behalf. A good business attorney may notice a small clause in a lease agreement that appears to be boilerplate, but is really negotiable. The savings from these discoveries will more often than not pay for the time it takes to have the leases reviewed.

Advisor. A good attorney is a trusted business advisor. While his or her focus is on the legal aspects of your decision making, business attorneys have the experience and savvy of general business practices and procedures that may be unfamiliar to you. This is where the partnering comes in. It's one thing to review an occasional contract; it's another to have an ongoing dialogue where your attorney is committed to the same type of business growth and objectives that you want to achieve.

Business structure. Your attorney can advise you about the best legal structure for the business. You may begin the business as a sole proprietorship, and then decide to incorporate. An attorney can help you evaluate this choice and can explain the pros and cons of different legal structures. While your CPA will have input based on the financial ramifications of various legal structures for a business, the attorney's viewpoint will focus both on liability issues and on common business practice for your industry.

Specialization. A general business attorney will have good basic knowledge about all of the potential legal issues that your business may encounter. There will be times, however, when referrals to specialists will be appropriate. Let's take a look at some of these specializations.

✓ *Labor law.* In our increasingly litigious society, issues of labor law have become highly specialized. Your attorney can help you in the preparation of a comprehensive, yet simple, employee handbook. This document will cover all of the basic expectations of the relationship between your company and the employee (including the right to fire "at will"). There are times, however, when even the best preparation will catch you unaware. Accusations of sexual harassment or racial discrimination, for example, may put your company in a precarious position—regardless of who is right or wrong. Your attorney will refer you to a labor law specialist who can shepherd you through the maze of employment law.

✓ *Intellectual property.* Do you want to trademark or patent something unique in your business? Again, your business attorney can probably handle the basics quite well, but you will want to go to an intellectual property attorney to draft underlying documents that will protect the intangible property.

✓ *Product liability.* We've seen huge companies file for bankruptcy protection as a result of aggressive product liability suits. If your company manufactures a product that can in any way harm its user, you need a product liability specialist. Much of this litigation is being handled by arbitration specialists today, so that may be another connection you can make.

✓ *Tax planning.* The joy of making a lot of money from the business is only diminished by the increased amount you will pay out in taxes. Your attorney can cover all of the basic tax planning for the company, but when it gets more sophisticated, it will be in both of your best interests to bring in a tax attorney. Most tax attorneys are CPAs as well, so they understand the accounting implications in depth.

Disability. A business owner's largest asset is usually his or her investment in the business. As the value of the business increases, you want to make sure that you are prepared for what happens if you become disabled. While disability insurance will pay you while you are unable to work, your attorney can help you strategize how to keep the business going in your absence. You may grant power of attorney to him or her so that the business can function even when you're not there. These are the necessary and serious conversations that must happen if you are the strategic planner for your business.

Estate planning.   The next level is estate planning. Again, given the proportionately large share of assets the business represents to you, your business attorney is in an excellent position to advise you on how to handle trusts and estates. In conjunction with a tax attorney, you may decide to set up trusts to shelter certain income while simultaneously preparing for your heirs.

How to find one.   The best way to find an attorney is to talk to other business owners and to network through your associations and local Chamber of Commerce. The element of *chemistry* is important with someone who can potentially become one of your most trusted advisors. Take time to get to know several possible candidates, then pick the one who has the ideal experience and legal and business connections. And make sure you like each other, because you may be destined to spend a lot of emotionally charged time together.

You can see through these examples that your business attorney can save you money, be a trusted advisor, and be a valued resource who can guide you to other legal professionals. Take your time to find the right fit—it will pay off substantially as you grow your business.

FIVE

MONEY— THE FUTURE

Chapter 46

The Valuation Process

At some point, you'll ask the question, "What is this business worth?" A valuation will lead you to the answer. Think of the valuation process as an exciting one where you will see an outside expert assess the cumulative blood, sweat, and tears that you've put into your business.

Old style. In years past, valuations were performed largely as a result of a company's balance sheet. In a traditional manufacturing company, for example, you would add up all the assets, subtract the liabilities, and the resulting net worth would be the stated value of the company. That worked in the bricks-and-mortar manufacturing environment of old, but that model doesn't work as well today. This issue has become complicated by the challenge of evaluating service businesses, which by nature are not asset-rich entities.

New style. The combination of service businesses and the knowledge economy makes valuations a challenging exercise. Professionals need to assess different variables, since hard assets are not a large part of the business. The starting point is cash flow, not assets, and valuation will largely be based on the future earnings power of the business. A professional appraiser will take into account current and projected cash flows, while concurrently assessing numerous aspects that are hard to assign and attach dollar values to.

Things such as the value of a customer list, market share, your location, your brand—anything proprietary—need to be factored into the decision. The valuing of these intangibles is subject to great interpretation. The accounting profession is currently wrestling with how to value these items that do not appear on a company's balance sheet. As futurists Edith Weiner and Arnold Brown discuss in *Insider's Guide to the Future,* the new economy is one where your employees, your customers, and your reputation are critical factors, and none of these is an asset that shows up on your balance sheet.

One of the things to think about is the lifetime value of your customers. For how long will they be your customers? What is the average annual revenue you will generate from these customers? Have you evaluated the profitability of these customers? This type of thought process can help you assess the value of the intangible assets in your business.

When you need a valuation.   In most situations, a formal valuation will not be necessary. There are several occasions, however, when a professional one will be necessary. First, you need one if you are planning to sell your business. An independent valuation will help you capture the highest price. Second, if you're soliciting equity investments from angels or other venture capitalists, a valuation will help determine the price set for the equity. Next, if you're planning to do an IPO, a valuation will be necessary as you price the equity for outside investors.

Another reason for a valuation has nothing to do with selling the business or raising equity—you'll need a valuation for estate planning purposes. By valuing your business, you'll be better prepared to do estate planning. Unlike the case of selling your business, you want to have a *lower* value in place when doing estate planning. By doing it yourself, you may inadvertently *overvalue* the business, and your heirs may be faced with substantial tax liability because you planned inappropriately.

When to bring in a professional.   As the business owner, you are actually in the best position to put a price against these intangible assets. Your experience and insights will carry more weight than those of an outside appraiser. That having been said, when you are selling the business or raising equity, an outside appraisal is virtually a necessity. Count on spending $10,000 to $15,000 and up for a professional valuation.

An interim step.   Not yet in a situation where you need a formal valuation, but want to validate your financial condition? A good interim solution is to hire a CPA firm to audit your financial statements. In so doing, you'll get a professional "seal of approval" that the figures you've presented are valid. This will be satisfactory for most banks and many other investors.

Solo management.   If you're the business owner/CEO/president and don't have other people sharing in the management of the company, much of the value is based on *you*. Much as you might be a genius at what you do, upon valuing your business, it will be readily apparent that the value plunges if you're no longer the person performing the service that you've been rendering all along. This is something to think about as you grow the business: Do you want to create depth greater than yourself?

Building management depth and a company that can flourish without you is a way to build equity in your company. This is a catch-22 for many business owners: After investing all the time and effort to build a business, if you want to build equity, *you* need to back off. If you don't, you will always be facing questions about whether the business is an enterprise, or whether it's just you.

In seeking expert advice for valuation services, here are a few resources that may be helpful.

✓ The International Business Brokers Association, (703) 437-7464, e-mail at IBBAInc@aol.com

✓ The Institute of Business Appraisers, (561) 732-3202, e-mail at iba@instbusapp.org

✓ The American Society of Appraisers, (703) 478-2228. This organization publishes the *Directory of Professional Appraisers* that contains more than 4,000 accredited appraisers, including approximately 1,700 business appraisers. The publication price is $12.95, which includes shipping within the United States. Call (800) 272-8258 to order.

Once you've received some referrals to appraisers, check references before moving forward with anyone. Make sure your appraiser has evaluated businesses like yours before, especially if your company is service- or knowledge-based.

Keep in mind that there is a lot about valuation that is extremely subjective. As we move more solidly into the knowledge economy, the value of the intangible assets of your business—your employees, your customers, your brand equity, and other important factors—is not easily measured. It's the dilemma we face as pioneers in this new information economy: trying to have others evaluate our new-style fluid businesses using the yardstick of old-style bricks-and-mortar industries. Until the measurement tools become more defined, it will be very much left to subjective interpretation.

Chapter 47

Investing Excess Cash

I magine the happy problem of generating such great profits that your business is literally rolling in cash! What do you do with this money so that you can generate your best return on investment?

Your first evaluation should focus on whether you want to temporarily invest in securities (stocks and bonds) to receive dividends or interest, or invest in the longer-term growth of the company. There are times when either strategy is appropriate. The important issue to consider is to make sure that your decision is strategically driven and not whimsical in nature.

Marketable securities. Let's say that you'll only have this excess cash for a short time, say six to nine months. After that, you'll be investing in a new advertising campaign for the business. For this short period, it's best to keep the funds safe and liquid (easily converted to cash). Marketable securities, such as U.S. Treasury bills or the highest-grade commercial paper, are excellent choices. (Commercial paper is a short-term IOU used to fund corporate working capital requirements.) To assure the most safety, invest in commercial paper with only the highest ratings. You'll not get the highest returns from these investments, but you will be invested in safe, liquid securities, where there is little market risk.

Medium term. If you can hold onto the cash a little longer, you can consider investing a portion of it in mutual funds, which may generate higher returns than the marketable securities. You have a little more market risk with mutual funds in that the net asset value can fluctuate, and you may be forced to liquidate before you are prepared to (which means the value of your investment could decrease, and you could lose money). Look at the fund history and the expense ratio paid to the fund manager, and find out when the fund goes ex-dividend (pays its dividends) in order to determine the optimum time to sell any shares.

The key to both short- and medium-term investments is to remember that unless it's the mainstay of your business, you're not in the business of being in the stock or bond markets. Think of both of these strategies as interim places to park excess cash until you can invest it back into the business.

Special shareholder dividend.   There may come a time when you just want to take out the excess cash. In this case, you may declare a special dividend and distribute the money to your shareholders. Check with your CPA about any tax implications, but in general, this is a good way to get cash out of the company and into your own hands.

Pension plans.   These are discussed in greater detail in the next chapter. You can make tax-deferred contributions into your 401(k) or Keogh plan. These funds are not commingled with other corporate funds, so this is a place within the company structure where you can build some tax-deferred returns.

Life insurance.   You may have been waiting until you generated enough cash to invest in life insurance policies. This strategy can protect the business if something happens to you. Life insurance can be structured to benefit both business partners as well as your heirs. And, if you purchase a whole life policy, you will be building cash value, tax-free, which you can borrow against in the future. Explore this option with your insurance broker.

Reinvest in the business.   After evaluating these different options, you may discover that you will get the best return on your excess cash by plowing the money back into the business. Here are some ideas:

✓ Invest in equipment that will improve the operating efficiency of your business. You may have been deferring this decision due to cash short-ages. With excess cash in hand, an equipment upgrade may enhance your productivity so that you see immediate returns on this investment.

✓ Expand your business by investing in a business that is complimentary to your core business. This may be either a business that is already up and running, or one that you decide to develop from startup. Evaluate every-thing, from the time involved with such a decision to finding the right managers to run it.

✓ Invest in a key officer or manager, whose presence will help you develop management depth in the company. This is often an area of resistance for small business owners, so do a cost-benefit analysis. For example, hiring the manager may be an $80,000-per-year chunk of money, but bringing on the right professional could enhance the overall valuation of the company.

In assessing any of these investments for your business, spend some time calculating potential return on investment. The process is simply to see what you'll make back over time by investing in new resources—people, products, or businesses—today. Run the numbers to determine the best outcome from each of the potential decisions, and work with your CPA if you are uncertain about how to evaluate them.

All of this circles back to the idea that any investment strategy is just that—strategic. Don't make haphazard decisions that might look great in the short run, but will cause you problems later. Think about your long-term goals for the business, and see where the luxury of excess cash can help you reach those strategic objectives.

Chapter 48

Retirement Planning

Many small business owners neglect the subject of retirement planning. What with marketing, sales strategies, and new product ideas, the subject of collecting a pension seems remote and unreal. Nonetheless, even a one-person company can establish a program where steady contributions will generate cash for the future.

Strategic importance. Your approach to retirement should be strategic, like your other major business planning issues. From a financial perspective, retirement plans involve three key components. First, this is a major employee benefit, whether it is just 1 person or a staff of 50. Contributions to a retirement plan are tax advantaged from the company's perspective as well as the employee's.

Second, once you commit to a retirement plan, you should be prepared to contribute every year. That means that your retirement obligation becomes an annual budget item.

Third, retirement plans are investment vehicles. The funds invested in your retirement plan are central to your financial future. Most people under 50 don't have confidence in receiving Social Security payments when they retire, so your company retirement plan becomes pivotal from a personal finance perspective.

Types. Many types of retirement plans exist, and you should check with your tax professional to confirm the details of the plans mentioned here, as well as any new ones that may have arisen since this writing.

Profit sharing. This is a flexible option where the company contributes a percentage of compensation to every employee's account every year. You're able to determine the percentage every year. In better years, you can contribute a higher percentage, while in years when profits are lower, the percentage contributions can be adjusted lower. Your company can contribute up to the lesser of 15 percent of salary or $30,000. Profit sharing is a great psychological boost at most companies. Your employees know that if the company does better, they will have a greater chance of a higher level of profit sharing. It's a subtle way to motivate people on an ongoing basis.

Many financial services firms have developed information packets on retirement options for small business owners. Fidelity Investments' free booklet, *Retirement Plans for Small Business,* is available by calling (800) 544-5373. Charles Schwab has a startup kit on Qualified Retirement Plans, available by calling (800) 540-8210. Another great place to start your research is the Internet; most financial services firms have extensive Web sites featuring their retirement products.

Money purchase. Your company contributes a percentage of compensation to each employee's account up to the lesser of $30,000 or 25 percent of salary. This percentage is fixed, and you must contribute the same percentage each year. As such, you don't have the flexibility of adjusting the percentage when you have higher or lower profits, as in the profit-sharing option.

Keogh. You can use either a profit-sharing or money-purchase option. Keoghs can be established only for sole proprietors or partnerships, so it is not an option for corporations. The percentage contributions are the same as in straight profit-sharing or money-purchase plans. If your Keogh has more than $100,000 in assets, you need to file the IRS Form 5500 EZ every year. This filing is due on July 31.

Defined benefit. If you are over the age of 50, you may be able to save even more money by using a defined benefit plan. This type of plan can be used by sole proprietors, partnerships, or corporations. Consult your tax or pension advisor to see if this approach is appropriate for your company.

Simplified employee pension (SEP). This plan, also frequently referred to as an SEP-IRA, is like the profit-sharing plan—your company contributes a percentage of salary to each employee's account. The percentage can vary from year to year and you can even skip a year. The contribution amount is also the same as a profit-sharing plan: the lesser of 15 percent of salary or $24,000. The trick with SEPs is that you must make contributions for everyone, including part-time employees. They have low startup and operating costs, and no IRS filings are necessary.

Traditional 401(k).   Your employees make pretax contributions into their accounts in the form of salary deferrals. Your company can match all, or part, or none of these contributions. For example, employees may contribute up to 6 percent of their compensation into the 401(k). A person making $50,000 can defer up to $3,000. He or she will pay income taxes on $47,000 in wages, as the $3,000 is deferred in the 401(k). If the company matches up to 3 percent, it will contribute an additional $1,500 to the employee's account.

Employee contributions are capped at $10,000 at this writing. The combined amount from the company and the employee cannot exceed the lesser of 25 percent of salary or $30,000. One of the challenges of 401(k)s is a discrimination clause. Higher-paid employees may be restricted on the amount they can contribute, if enough lower-paid employees do not participate. Your company must file the IRS Form 5500 annually.

If your plan allows, make your retirement contribution early in the year. For example, in some plans, retirement contributions for the 1998 tax year can be made until tax filing day on April 15, 1999. Savvy entrepreneurs, however, make at least part of their contribution in January 1998, gaining almost 16 months of interest. Over time, this strategy can have a significant positive impact on your retirement investment as interest accrues. Check with your financial and tax advisors to see if your plan allows this, and how you can maximize your retirement savings.

SIMPLE 401(k).   SIMPLE plans, or Savings Incentive Match Plan for Employees of Small Employers, were authorized by the government's Small Business Job Protection Act of 1996 for employers of 100 or fewer employees. In the SIMPLE 401(k) plan, your company contributes 2 percent of all eligible workers' pay, up to $4,800. Or, it can match up to 3 percent against employee contributions. Employees need to have made at least $5,000 in the previous 2 years, and participants are immediately vested. Again, you need to file the Form 5500 annually.

SIMPLE IRA.   This option does not require any IRS filings. As in the SIMPLE 401(k), your company can choose to contribute up to 3 percent for elective matches or 2 percent across the board for all eligible employees, up to $6,000. Again, employees need to have made at least $5,000 in the previous 2 years, and participants are immediately vested.

Evaluation. The SIMPLE IRA has received a lot of attention since its inception in 1997. Keep in mind that the $6,000 annual maximum is $3,500 lower than the $9,500 cap in a traditional 401(k), and substantially less than the possible $30,000 in a Keogh. A SIMPLE IRA may be a good solution in a business with a lot of lower-paid employees (such as a restaurant or health club) who may not be interested in participating in a retirement plan. Neither SIMPLE plan is allowable if you have another retirement plan in place.

As you can see, these plans have many financial subtleties that make them complicated to evaluate. We strongly encourage you to do some preliminary homework on your own, then consult your accountant, a fee-only financial planner, or a pension consultant to help you wade through the options. These professionals often have software tools that enable you to calculate several "what if" scenarios. After weighing the pros and cons, you'll come up with the best plan for your company, and you will be setting the groundwork for protecting your financial future.

Chapter 49

Hypergrowth

A s you're growing your business, you may face a moment where your idea turns into a phenomenally successful product or service. This surge means that you'll likely reach a crossroads: Will you let the company grow at a regular, *normal* rate, or will you push it to take off like a rocket? If you shoot for the stars, you're in for a thrilling ride filled with high-stakes risks and rewards. Welcome to the world of hypergrowth.

Bold vision. The concept of hypergrowth begins in your mind. As the business owner, you must have a vision so clear, so big and bold that it's alive and three-dimensional at all times. You also need to be able to communicate this vision to anyone and everyone, starting with your employees. Hypergrowth doesn't occur solo—you need a team of people to support your growth and goals on an ongoing basis. While loyal independent contractors may be good contributors, your in-house staff has the bigger vested interest.

Enthusiasm. If you aren't continually 150-percent excited about your vision, how can you expect people to follow suit? You may find yourself turning into an enthusiastic maniac, but this energy is contagious. Expressing this excitement on an ongoing basis will do wonders to bring your dream into reality. As your coworkers and customers climb aboard the vision, the spirit multiplies geometrically, and the group energy propels the company through both the good times and the challenges.

Share the vision. Everyone from your chief operating officer to your receptionist should fully understand the company's vision for the future. Place reminders of the vision everywhere. Come up with a catchy phrase and logo that instantly triggers goal recognition by every member of your staff. And don't stop there—your customers and vendors will know about it, too. You want to build a vision with an identity that's instantly recognizable. What is your equivalent of the golden arches or Nike's swoosh?

Constant benchmarking.   The vision then must translate into goals. What must happen in order to reach the aggressive goals you are setting? This is a function of determined and focused planning where *everyone* owns the end result. Hypergrowth does not occur haphazardly; it's the result of creating and working a dynamic, forward-thinking plan. You'll establish rigorous benchmarks, against which you will measure your company's actual performance. By monitoring your plan against actual results on a frequent basis, you'll be able to see early on if you're going off course.

Cash to grow.   Hypergrowth takes a lot of money. You've learned about the working capital cycle, and what to do when you're awaiting customer payments and you need to meet payroll. Hypergrowth is a different ball game. You're nearly always going to owe someone something, so get used to borrowing on a regular, and often expensive, basis. Banks are not necessarily comfortable with the idea of companies growing at the speed of light, so you cannot rely on them as your only source.

On the other hand, if you've established a good relationship with your bank, and have played by the rules as a responsible borrower, you'll have a greater potential for success with your banker. Remember the perspective of bankers: They're looking for assurances that the loan advanced to your company will be paid back. In any case, the patchwork approach will be critical to your success in rapidly growing your business. You'll rely on everything from bootstrapping to creative financing to get to your goal.

The best employees.   Excellence is virtually always a prerequisite for phenomenal growth. Think about it—how can you expect to achieve your goals if, for example, your attention to detail is sloppy or your investment in your people is minimal? In committing to hypergrowth, you're committing to excellence. You're sending the message that you're going to be the best, and this will be reflected in all aspects of your business.

This is best exemplified in sales. The best salespeople love what they sell and love the interaction with every potential customer. They live, sleep, and breathe the business in such a way that having a casual conversation with a prospect can excite that person into buying. Invest in the best training, commit yourself to calling on the top accounts—these are things that will be expected as standard levels of performance.

In a hypergrowth company, there's no room for laggards. *All* of your employees need to be top performers who "get it" about your vision. One of the small business challenges is hiring the right people for the jobs that need to be done. We often compromise, thinking that we won't be able to find anyone better. That perspective alone could kill a plan for hypergrowth. Objectively assess the skill levels of your staff, and make adjustments where necessary.

A word about family.   Most business owners are already wrapped up in their businesses. When you transfer into hypergrowth mode, your involvement will become even more intense. Do your family a favor by sharing the dream with them, and explaining what you'll need for support during this exciting time. We tend to take advantage of family by ignoring these connections when we're wrapped up in work. Instead of that, make sure you carve out some family time each week—even if it is only Sunday brunch—so that you keep those relationships intact.

The decision to engage in hypergrowth is entirely yours. You'll need an unwavering, strong desire that translates into action. Talk it over with your trusted advisors and business confidants before you start. Clearly assess all the risks, as well as the rewards. Then once the rocket takes off, hang on. You're business will never be the same.

Chapter 50

Exit Strategies

Long term, what do you want out of your business? Do you want to sell it at age 50, or work until you are 110 years old? Seriously, when you build a company, you need to think about what happens down the road. How you move on—selling all or part of the business—is called an *exit strategy*. As your business grows, you need to think about how you will get out.

We introduced the concept of exit strategy in the chapters on venture capital financing. Angels and traditional venture capitalists look at investing in your business to make impressive financial returns—but only if there is an exit strategy, or way that they can get their investment out after a 5- to 10-year period. Take this concept and apply it to yourself: If you look 5 to 10 years forward, what does the business look like—especially if you want to move on?

Building equity. Most discussions about exit strategy revolve around building equity in the business. As was highlighted in Chapter 46, valuations are necessary to determine the overall worth of the company. Service- and knowledge-based businesses are particularly sensitive to the concept of equity valuation, as there are few hard assets to measure.

You and the business. This is where the question of "Are *you* the business?" becomes important. If you're a consultant or an accountant, for example, you *are* the business. You need to work in order to make money. If this is the case, you have limited options as you get older, because the business relies on you. This is a perfectly acceptable strategy if you've been able to earn a sizable amount of money to invest for retirement. In that case, you can think of your business as generating large amounts of current cash flow to the exclusion of building equity.

Solo exit. It's virtually impossible to exit a business if it revolves solely around you. Of course, you may be able to sell it to a larger company, but *you* will be part of the package. Consider a David-and-Goliath scenario: You have an enormously successful public relations business, highlighted by a proprietary group of contacts. A much larger competitor has eyed your company for some time—has even been beaten in competition by your strong performance. The larger PR firm wants to buy your business. What they're really buying is *you* and *your contact list.* In the best-case scenario, you'll be paid your asking sales price and, in return, the larger firm gets your commitment to work for them—doing what you've been doing on your own—for the next five years.

Succession planning.   If you want to build equity, start thinking about succession. The reality of building a management team is a source of anxiety for most business owners. Going from being the chief cook and bottle washer to committing to key managers and officers can be scary. Get over this fear. Bring on the best people you can find, and include them in your vision.

Over time, determine who will be the best successor as CEO. Start mentoring and grooming that person to take over in three to five years. During this time, you can delegate more responsibilities and see how it feels to have someone else in a key role.

Build a product line.   Another option is to make a strategic decision to buy or create a product line. Building these sales is an effective way to build equity. As the product becomes a more significant percentage of total revenue, your company's valuation will increase. This happens because *you* are no longer the main source of revenue. Begin today to think about how you can build product into your business.

Partial sale.   In formulating your strategies for exit, you may choose to sell part of the company and invest the proceeds in something entirely different. Keep in mind that selling options range from *part* of the business to *all* of the business. In some cases, the sale of a divisional crown jewel may be better for your bank account than selling the entire company.

Contemplating an exit strategy may seem far removed from your experiences of the day-to-day business life you're currently leading. Casting an eye to the future, however, can bring clarity to both your short-term and long-term plans, and can put both struggles and achievements in perspective.

As we close this final chapter of *The Small Business Money Guide,* we encourage you to return to these pages as your business evolves. Our goal is to show you that money is just one of many business tools—but an important one to understand and control. Working with any unfamiliar tool is a bit uncomfortable at first. With practice, however, you soon make the change from awkward handling to using the tool as a natural extension of your abilities. It's the same with money. Once you learn to use money effectively in your business, it will become a natural part of the entrepreneurial toolbox you use to build your vision.

Resources

In addition to the resources listed in this section, we encourage you to check out the *Working Solo Sourcebook* (also published by John Wiley & Sons, Inc.), which features a user-friendly collection of more than 1,200 valuable business resources.

Books

Applegarth, Ginger. *Wake Up and Smell the Money: Fresh Starts at Any Age—and Any Season of Your Life.* New York: Viking, 1999.

Bangs, David H., Jr. *The Cash-Flow Control Guide.* Chicago, IL: Dearborn Trade/Upstart, 1994.

Blechman, Bruce, and Jay Conrad Levinson. *Guerrilla Financing: Alternative Techniques to Finance Any Small Business.* Boston: Houghton Mifflin, 1991.

Blum, Laurie. *Free Money for Small Businesses and Entrepreneurs,* 4th ed. New York: John Wiley & Sons, 1995.

Career Press editors. *Business Finance for the Numerically Challenged.* Franklin Lakes, NJ: Career Press, 1997.

Cohen, William A. *The Entrepreneur and the Small Business Problem Solver.* New York: John Wiley & Sons, 1990.

Coltman, Michael M. *Understanding and Managing Financial Information: The Non-Financial Manager's Guide.* Self-Counsel Business Series. British Columbia: International Self-Counsel Press, 1993.

Daily, Frederick W. *Tax Savvy for Small Business: Year-Round Tax Advice for Small Businesses.* Berkeley, CA: Nolo Press, 1997.

Dawson, George M. *Borrowing to Build Your Business: Getting Your Banker to Say "Yes."* Chicago, IL: Dearborn Trade/Upstart, 1997.

Dumouchel, J. Robert. *Government Assistance Almanac: 1997–1998,* 11th ed. Detroit: Omnigraphics, 1997.

Entrepreneur Media. *The Entrepreneur Magazine Guide to Raising Money.* New York: John Wiley & Sons, 1998.

Flanagan, Lawrence. *The Money Connection: Where & How to Apply for Business Loans.* Grants Pass, OR: Oasis Press, 1995.

Graphic Artist's Guild Handbook of Pricing & Ethical Guidelines. Cincinnati, OH: North Light Books, 1997.

Hemphill, Barbara. *Taming the Paper Tiger.* Washington, DC: Kiplinger, 1997.

Leonard, Robin. *Credit Repair.* Berkeley, CA: Nolo Press, 1996.

Listner, Kate, and Tom Harnish. *Finding Money: The Small Business Guide to Financing.* A Wiley Small Business Edition. New York: John Wiley & Sons, 1995.

Lonier, Terri. *The Frugal Entrepreneur.* New Paltz, NY: Portico Press, 1996.

Lonier, Terri. *Smart Strategies for Growing Your Business.* New York: John Wiley & Sons, 1999.

Lonier, Terri. *Working Solo.* New York: John Wiley & Sons, 1998.

Lonier, Terri. *Working Solo Sourcebook.* New York: John Wiley & Sons, 1998.

Mancuso, Joseph R. *How to Get a Business Loan (Without Signing Your Life Away).* New York: Simon & Schuster, 1994.

Mancuso, Joseph R. *Mancuso's Small Business Basics.* Naperville, IL: Sourcebooks, 1998.

Nelson, Bob, and Ken Blanchard. *1001 Ways to Reward Employees.* New York: Workman, 1994.

O'Hara, Patrick D. *SBA Microloan & Specialty Loan Handbook.* A Wiley Small Business Edition. New York: John Wiley & Sons, 1996.

Penwell, Tracy L. *The Credit Process: A Guide for Small Business Owners.* Federal Reserve Bank of New York.

Placencia, Jose, Bruce Weige, and Don Oliver. *Business Owner's Guide to Accounting and Bookkeeping.* Grants Pass, OR: Oasis Press, 1997.

Sitarz, Daniel. *Simplified Small Business Accounting.* Carbondale, IL: Nova Publishing, 1995.

Stern, Linda. *Money Smart Secrets for the Self-Employed: Make More and Keep More When You Work for Yourself.* New York: Random House Reference & Info Publishing, 1997.

Stoltz, William J. *Start Up Financing.* Franklin Lakes, NJ: Career Press, 1997.

Tomzack, Mary E. *Tips and Traps When Buying a Franchise.* New York: McGraw-Hill, 1994.

Weiner, Edith, and Arnold Brown. *Insider's Guide to the Future.* Greenwich, CT: Boardroom, Inc., 1997.

Weinstein, Grace. *Financial Savvy for the Self-Employed.* New York: Henry Holt, 1996.

Winninger, Thomas J. *Price Wars: A Strategy Guide to Winning the Battle for the Customer.* Rocklin, CA: Prima Publishing, 1995.

Yegge, Wilbur M. *Self-Defense Finance for Small Business.* New York: John Wiley & Sons, 1995.

Zobel, Jan. *Minding Her Own Business: The Self-Employed Woman's Guide to Taxes and Recordkeeping.* Oakland, CA: East Hill Press, 1997.

Periodicals and Pamphlets

ABC's of Borrowing. Publication #FM01. U.S. Small Business Administration, P.O. Box 46521, Denver, CO 80201-46521. (800) 827-5722. What to expect when borrowing money for your small business.

American Banker. One State Street Plaza, New York, NY 10004. (212) 803-8333. A leader among the established daily financial services newspapers.

Budgeting in a Small Service Firm. Publication #FM08. U.S. Small Business Administration, P.O. Box 46521, Denver, CO 80201-46521. (800) 827-5722. A booklet that shows you how to set up and maintain your business' financial records.

Business Week. The McGraw-Hill Companies, 1221 Avenue of the Americas, New York, NY 10020. (212) 512-2000. Weekly business news analysis and commentary.

Entrepreneur. 2392 Morse Avenue, Irvine, CA 92614. (714) 261-2325; (800) 274-6229; www.entrepreneurmag.com. Information, news, and stories on and for the SOHO workforce.

Forbes. 60 Fifth Avenue, New York, NY 10011. (800) 888-9896; www.forbes.com. Biweekly business and financial news and information.

Fortune. Time and Life Building, Rockefeller Center, New York, NY 10020. (800) 280-8205.

Inc. 38 Commercial Wharf, Boston, MA 02110. (800) 234-0999; www.inc.com. Monthly small business news and information.

Money. Time and Life Building, Rockefeller Center, New York, NY 10020. (800) 280-8205; www.money.com.

The New York Times. 229 West 43rd Street, New York, NY 10036. (800) 698-4637; www.nytimes.com. Daily business and world news.

The Pricing Advisor Newsletter. The Pricing Advisor, Inc., 3277 Roswell Road, Suite 620, Atlanta, GA 30305. (770) 509-9933. Monthly newsletter that focuses on pricing strategies and policies.

Success. 733 Third Avenue, New York, NY 10017. (212) 883-7100. Monthly business magazine for the entrepreneurially minded.

U.S. Small Business Administration's Borrower's Guide. U.S. Small Business Administration, 409 Third Street SW, 6th floor, Washington, DC 20416. (800)U-ASK-SBA. A guide to small business loan programs available through the SBA.

U.S. Small Business Administration's Lender's Guide. U.S. Small Business Administration, 409 Third Street SW, 6th floor, Washington, DC 20416. (800)U-ASK-SBA. A guide to lenders and financial institutions that serve the small business sector.

A Venture Capital Primer for Small Business. Publication #FM05. U.S. Small Business Administration, P.O. Box 46521, Denver, CO 80201-46521. (800) 827-5722. Booklet that helps you understand and secure venture capital.

The Wall Street Journal. 200 Liberty Street, New York, NY 10281. (800) 568-7625; www.wsj.com. Leading daily business newspaper, with accompanying Web site.

Web Sites

The best way to begin your online research is with one of the powerful Internet search engines, such as Yahoo (www.yahoo.com), Lycos (www.lycos.com), Alta Vista (www.altavista.com), or Infoseek (www.infoseek.com). Following are some specific sites that offer valuable information on small business and money matters.

American Express Small Business, www.americanexpress.com/smallbusiness. Small business financial news and information.

CNBC, www.cnbc.com. A leader in business news.

CNN/fn, http://cnnfn.com. A leader in business and financial news.

Dun & Bradstreet Information Services, www.dnb.com. Credit, collection, and data protection information.

Intuit, www.quicken.com/small_business. A small business site with business management advice, from the makers of the top-rated financial management software for small business.

SBA Online, U.S. Small Business Administration, www.sba.gov. Central clearinghouse of information on federal programs for small business, including financial assistance.

Index

About the Authors

TERRI LONIER is the nation's leading expert on solo entrepreneurs. As president of Working Solo, Inc., she advises clients including Microsoft, Hewlett-Packard, Apple Computer, Bank of America, Intuit, and Seagram's on how best to access and communicate with the rapidly growing small business and small office/home office (SOHO) market.

Her highly acclaimed Working Solo resources—including books, audiotapes, Web site (www.workingsolo.com), monthly e-mail newsletter, and seminars—offer information and inspiration to thousands of solo entrepreneurs worldwide. (For details, send an e-mail to info@workingsolo.com, or call (800) 222-7656.)

A successful entrepreneur since 1978, Ms. Lonier is an in-demand business speaker on entrepreneurial topics and a frequent media guest. Her work has been featured in the *New York Times, Wall Street Journal, Inc., Fast Company, Business Week,* and other leading business publications, as well as on CNBC, CNN/fn, and radio programs nationwide. She was honored as the keynote speaker at the First International Conference of Women in Business in Tokyo.

Ms. Lonier lives in New Paltz, New York, with her husband, Robert Sedestrom.

LISA M. ALDISERT is a management consultant and executive coach who develops business and leadership strategies. She offers a unique blend of financial acumen, trends analysis, and strategic planning to corporate and entrepreneurial clients. She helps them identify and implement new opportunities in today's constantly changing environment. Her work as a senior consultant with the leading futurist consulting group, Weiner, Edrich, Brown, places her on the cutting edge of trends analysis.

Ms. Aldisert spent 16 years in corporate finance, sales, and financial management at two of the country's largest banks. She successfully made the transition from banker to business owner by integrating the banking experience with the vision and energy of an entrepreneur. She has owned and operated an apparel manufacturing company, and was the founding president of a business association for entrepreneurs.

Ms. Aldisert is a frequent speaker on strategic business topics. She has been on the faculty of the Small Business Center at the Fashion Institute of Technology and the Cornell University School of Industrial and Labor Relations.

Ms. Aldisert lives in New York City with her husband, Batt Johnson.

For further information, please visit her Web site at www.lisaaldisert.com.